WHAT'S MY
TYPE?

WHAT'S MY Type?

100+ QUIZZES to Help You

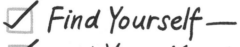 Find Yourself—
 and Your Match!

NATASHA BURTON

Adams Media
New York London Toronto Sydney New Delhi

Adams Media
An Imprint of Simon & Schuster, Inc.
57 Littlefield Street
Avon, Massachusetts 02322

First Adams Media trade paperback edition February 2020

ADAMS MEDIA and colophon are trademarks of Simon & Schuster.

For information about special discounts for bulk purchases, please contact Simon & Schuster Special Sales at 1-866-506-1949 or business@simonandschuster.com.

The Simon & Schuster Speakers Bureau can bring authors to your live event. For more information or to book an event contact the Simon & Schuster Speakers Bureau at 1-866-248-3049 or visit our website at www.simonspeakers.com.

Interior design by Julia Jacintho

Manufactured in the United States of America

10 9 8 7 6 5 4 3 2 1

Library of Congress Cataloging-in-Publication Data has been applied for.

ISBN 978-1-5072-1274-5
ISBN 978-1-5072-1275-2 (ebook)

For Ella and Aden

Acknowledgments

First, the people who made this book possible: my agent, Ariana Phillips, and the incredible team at JVNLA. The team at Adams Media—Rebecca Thomas, who offered me this project, and Sarah Doughty, my editor. I appreciate you all so much, especially for your thoughtful guidance along the way. Thank you. Here's to future projects together!

I'll always be indebted to Elizabeth Evans, my first (rock star!) agent, and Brendan O'Neill, who gave me my very first book deal. I also want to thank Laura Biagi and Christine Dore for their roles in my past book projects.

Thank you to my husband, Greg, for encouraging me to take on this project even when I needed to work at night and on weekends. Thank you to my daughter, Ella, for being patient as I answered emails and jotted down ideas on my phone. Thank you to my baby boy, Aden, for napping in your crib so I could write in the mornings while you slept. You guys allow me to continue my writing work along with my life's work—our family.

Contents

Introduction

Choosing the ideal romantic partner can feel like playing the ultimate game of chance. You need to be in the right place (or swipe right) at the right time, in the right frame of mind—you get the idea. So how do you know when you have met the best match? The answer is actually quite simple: You have to know *yourself*. Being an expert on your own beliefs, interests, relationship needs, and more gives you the clarity to choose the best possible partner—and be the best possible partner in return.

And that's where *What's My Type?* comes in: Here you'll discover more than one hundred fun, easy, and illuminating quizzes to help you better understand yourself, along with what you need and want in a potential partner. With quizzes ranging from straightforward multiple-choice options, to open-ended explorations of different themes like family and marriage, *What's My Type?* allows you to use past experiences, present values, and future goals to identify what you cherish in yourself—and what you cherish in your relationships. But before you dive in, take a look at the next section on how to use this book. The information here will help you gain as much insight as possible from each quiz you take!

So, are you ready to learn more about, well, *you*? You're sure to walk away knowing your own answer to the question, "What's my type?"

How to Use This Book

Think of this book as your partner in crime on your journey to finding your perfect match. As you go through the quizzes on the pages that follow, you'll uncover new understanding about yourself—and about the ideal partner for you. Read on for more details about each quiz type, from how to complete each one, to how to use your results to supercharge your love life.

ABOUT THE QUIZZES

The quizzes in this book are divided into three parts: past, present, and future. Part 1 deals with past experiences that may play a part in who you are now and what you may look for in a potential partner. Part 2 focuses on your beliefs, personal strengths, and other elements of the here and now that factor into your best romantic match. Part 3 is where you will find quizzes dealing with the goals and dreams you have for your future—and the kind of partner you would want to share that future with.

You can start at the beginning of Part 1 and work your way through the quizzes in each part, flip to the quizzes that jump out at you, or focus on specific topics. This book was designed for *you*: Tailor the content to your unique needs. And as you work through the different quizzes, take note of any questions that spark a particularly strong emotion or memory. These questions can be the most revealing.

However you decide to progress through this book, also be sure to review the short wrap-up section after each completed quiz. Here you'll find a recap of the important themes in the quiz, as well as instructions for how you can apply your results directly to your own journey toward love.

Quiz Types

The quizzes are also divided into six different types: Open-Ended, Fill In the Blank, This or That, Never Have You Ever/Do You Ever/ Would You Ever, Check It Off, and Multiple Choice. You may find yourself cracking up recalling some of your more cringeworthy dates on one page, then analyzing how your parents' relationship has shaped your own romantic philosophies on the next. Read on for more information about each quiz type.

- **Open-Ended.** These are a straightforward series of interview-like questions for you to answer. Typically, the content in these quizzes is deep, and may require a bit of room to write. Grab a notebook to jot down your answers.

- **Fill In the Blank.** Similar to the Open-Ended quizzes, these often center on deep topics, but provide a little more guidance to steer your self-reflection. Write your answers on the lines provided.

- **This or That.** These quizzes have you choose between two options in an "either/or" question. Don't overthink the choices: The point is to go with your gut and see what you might discover about yourself. Circle (or underline or check off) the option in each scenario that resonates most with you.

- **Never Have You Ever/Do You Ever/Would You Ever.** A nod to the games that you likely played in your younger days, these quizzes present quick takes on your past, present, or future. They may highlight what situations you've avoided (intentionally or not), encourage you to take a look at your current choices, or help you get creative about your romantic desires. You can check off the options that apply (or, in some cases, don't apply) to you—or write yes or no beside each option.

- **Check It Off.** These quizzes provide premade lists of options. Check off what applies to you in each list. Your choices may reveal a more concrete picture of thoughts or feelings you may be surprised by. Each quiz also offers blank spaces for you to add your own options to the list so you can tailor it to your unique situation.
- **Multiple Choice.** In these quizzes, you're given different options (typically around three per question) to get you thinking. Circle the option in each question that resonates most with you.

LET'S DO THIS!

Now that you've taken a closer look at the different types of quizzes you'll find in this book, it's time to dive in! Start your journey now to discover everything you need to know about yourself—and your type.

Part 1

PAST

Everyone begins each romantic relationship with a history—even if you may think you don't have a "significantly" storied past. From your relationships with family members and friends, to crushes and longer-term unions, your experiences have shaped who you are and how you relate to others. Understanding your own past—mining it for the clues and context of what you have wanted in relationships, who you have been as a partner, and why you've made certain romantic choices—is the key to your present and future connections.

The quizzes in this part will guide you to better understand how your own family dynamics and relationship role models have influenced you, and how past romantic and nonromantic experiences have shaped your outlook on love. Use this opportunity to dig deeper into your past (with an open mind!). By thinking critically and candidly about where you've been, you'll be better equipped to get where you want to go.

Your Relationship Role Models

Write your answers on the lines provided.

In the past, the relationship you most admired in your family was:

_____

_____

In the past, the relationship you most admired within your friend group was:

_____

_____

In the past, the relationship you most admired from celebrity/pop culture was:

_____

_____

In the past, the relationship you most admired from history was:

_____

_____

In the past, the relationship you most admired from books/movies/TV shows was: _____

_____

These couples have _____ in common.

You still admire/no longer admire the relationships you've listed because:

_____

_____

You've always admired couples who:

_____

_____

You've never wanted to be like couples who:

_____

_____

You've compared your own relationships to:

_____

_____

You've wanted to emulate qualities like _____
in your relationships in the past.

These role models likely had a big part in shaping your views of love and relationships, from what you desire in your own romantic relationships, to what you want to avoid. Use this information to better understand your unique romantic outlook and expectations.

When You Were Younger, You Were Sure You Were Going to Marry...

Check off each option that applies to you. Fill in the names and add your own options on the lines provided.

☐ From a TV show or movie: _____

☐ From elementary school: _____

☐ From middle school: _____

☐ From high school: _____

☐ From your family's social circle: _____

☐ From college: _____

☐ From celebrity culture: _____

☐ From work: _____

☐ From _____: _____

☐ From _____: _____

Do you notice any patterns or outliers in the types of people you wrote in your responses? These might provide clues to the qualities or personality types you gravitate toward, even in just a crush capacity.

Lessons from Your Parents' Marriage

Write your answers on a separate piece of paper.

1. How would you describe your parents' marriage in a few words?

2. If your parents are still together, what do you think is the key to their success?

3. If your parents are not together, how do you understand this decision?

4. Do you think your parents were/are happy in their relationship?

5. What's the biggest takeaway you received about love from your parents?

6. What wisdom did your parents share with you about partnership and/or marriage (either directly or through their actions)?

7. Would you want your own partnership and/or marriage to emulate your parents' relationship? Why, or why not?

8. If you have stepparents, how has seeing these different relationships between your parents and stepparents shaped your perspective of partnership?

9. What do you think your parents should have done differently in their relationship?

Your parents' relationship(s) has a major influence on your own future partnership. Analyzing what worked/works (or didn't/doesn't work) for them can provide clues to what you seek out in your own romantic relationships, and why—as well as providing helpful insights into what makes a lasting relationship.

How Were You Loved?

Circle the option in each question that best applies to you.

1. What level of physical affection was present in your household when you were a child?
   a. A lot of affection (lots of hugs, kisses, etc.)
   b. A decent amount of affection (some hugs, kisses, etc.)
   c. Not a lot of affection (few hugs, kisses, etc.)

2. How frequently was emotional affection and affirmation (e.g., saying "I love you") expressed?
   a. All of the time
   b. Pretty often
   c. Sometimes or rarely

3. Did your parents offer the same level of affection to you, or did one offer more than the other?
   a. One parent offered more than the other
   b. Both parents offered the same amount, it was close to equal, or I lived in a one-parent household

4. Did you crave love and affection from one parent more than the other?
   a. Yes, from my _____
   b. No

5. How did your parent(s) react when you were upset or crying?
   a. They held me close and helped me through it
   b. They told me to buck up
   c. They started crying along with me

6. Do you feel like your parents were sensitive to your needs as a child?
   a.   Yes, for the most part
   b.   Not always, but they did their best
   c.   No, not really

7. How were you expected to express your love to your parents and other family members?
   a.   I wasn't taught that you needed to
   b.   I was taught that you could express love when you felt like it
   c.   I was taught when to express love (give hugs, say "I love you," etc.)

8. Do you see yourself as a loving and affectionate person?
   a.   Yes
   b.   No
   c.   Kind of: _____ (explain)

9. Do you wish your parents had expressed love differently (either the way they expressed it or how frequently)?
   a.   Yes
   b.   No
   c.   It's complicated: _____ (explain)

The level of affection and love you received from your parents growing up sheds light on what you're used to, and thus what you may expect from a future partner. You may want the same level of affection that you experienced as a child, or you may want more or less, depending on how you feel now as you look back on this aspect of your past.

When's the Last Time You...

Write your answers on the lines provided.

Laughed until you cried: _____

_____

Cried because you were sad: _____

_____

Felt overwhelmed: _____

_____

Fell in love: _____

_____

Felt grateful: _____

_____

Felt disappointed in yourself: _____

_____

Felt disappointed by someone else: _____

_____

Felt proud of yourself: _____

_____

Felt sure of yourself: _____

_____

Totally embarrassed yourself: _____

_____

Overreacted about something: _____

_____

Made a big mistake: _____

_____

Apologized to someone: _____

_____

Admitted you were wrong: _____

_____

This quiz helps you to get in touch with a whole range of feelings and allows you to gauge your reactions to the moments in your life that triggered emotional release. How many of these emotions came as a result of your relationships, romantic or otherwise? In what ways might you work toward being more in tune with these emotions (and effectively expressing them) in your relationships going forward?

Influences That Shaped Your Views on Love and Romance

Check off each option that applies to you. Fill in the names and add your own options to the list on the lines provided.

☐ Your parents' relationship(s)

☐ Your grandparents' relationships

☐ Your friends

☐ Your siblings

☐ Your past relationships

☐ Movies/TV shows like:

_____

☐ Fictional stories like:

_____

☐ Self-help books like:

_____

☐ Conversations you've had with:

_____

☐ _____

☐ _____

Your relationship worldview is ever changing—influenced by people you've dated, books you've read, and more. But understanding how you got to where you are now can show you what factors in your life hold the most weight in shaping your beliefs about love. Consider what factors deserve more or less influence on your beliefs.

Prospects You Were More Likely to Reject

Circle the option in each scenario that resonates most with you.

In the past, you were more likely to reject someone who...

WAS: ○ Too good for you   ○ Not good enough for you

WAS: ○ Too boring   ○ Too dangerous

WAS: ○ Too good looking   ○ Not good looking enough

WAS: ○ Too inexperienced in bed   ○ Too adventurous in bed

WAS: ○ Too different from you   ○ Too similar to you

WAS: ○ Too nice   ○ Too abrasive

HAD: ○ Bad personal style   ○ Bad grammar

HAD: ○ Irritating texting habits   ○ Irritating table manners

HAD: ○ Bad teeth   ○ Bad hair

HAD: ○ Few books in their home   ○ Few toiletries in their home

Everyone has standards for the people they date, as well as individual preferences and pet peeves. Use this quiz as a starting point for thinking about why you've written people off in the past, and whether some reasons should be reevaluated—or given more weight in present or future relationships.

Dating History Edition

Check off each option that you *haven't* experienced.

☐ Been on a real date

☐ Tried online dating

☐ Gotten set up

☐ Asked someone on a date

☐ Turned down a date

☐ Stood someone up

☐ Been stood up

☐ Canceled on a date at the last minute

☐ Asked a friend out

☐ Asked a friend's ex out

☐ Slept with someone before going on a date

How many of these "nevers" did you check off? How do you feel about not having experienced them in the past? If there are any situations you're curious about experiencing, spend some time thinking about why they piqued your interest.

Love Advice You'd Give Your Past Self

Write your answers on a separate piece of paper.

1. When you had your first crush...

2. When you experienced your first heartbreak...

3. When it was prom night...

4. When you went on your first date...

5. When you didn't listen to your parents' advice...

6. When you were in college...

7. When you had that summer fling...

8. When you had sex for the first time...

9. When you got dumped...

10. When you realized someone wasn't "The One"...

11. When you got your first rejection...

You're savvier than you think when it comes to love—and when it comes to yourself. Because of where you've been—whether it has been secret crushes or a major breakup—you have knowledge about romance and relationships. So, remember to use your hindsight to your advantage.

Stereotypes You've Been Attracted To

Check off each option that applies to you, and add your own options to the list on the lines provided.

- ☐ The athlete
- ☐ The goth
- ☐ The preppy person
- ☐ The über-religious person
- ☐ The atheist
- ☐ The sender of unsolicited raunchy pictures
- ☐ The salt-of-the-earth type
- ☐ The activist
- ☐ The free spirit

- ☐ The ultra-experienced lover
- ☐ The slacker
- ☐ The musician
- ☐ The booty-call texter
- ☐ The perpetual child
- ☐ The friend with benefits
- ☐ The Paleo devotee
- ☐ _____
- ☐ _____

In addition to being a fun (or cringey) trip down memory lane, looking back on some of the good—and not-so-good—characters you've had the hots for in the past can provide insight into why certain traits have intrigued you. Are any of these traits worth kicking to the curb going forward?

Relationships You Were Most Likely to Have

Circle the option in each scenario that resonates most with you.

You've most likely...

HAD: O A casual booty call   O An intense love

HAD: O A long-distance relationship   O A cohabitating relationship

HAD: O A friend with benefits   O Zero friendship component

HAD: O A monogamous relationship   O An open relationship

HAD: O A hot and heavy relationship   O A comfortable relationship

HAD: O An insecure relationship   O A certain relationship

HAD: O A controlling love   O A codependent love

HAD: O A trophy relationship   O A secret relationship

HAD: O A convenient relationship   O An overly demanding relationship

Your relationship history shows a lot about the type of partner you may have been in the past (commitment avoidant, easily smitten, drama-driven, etc.)—or the type of partner you were drawn to. Are any of these partnerships the kinds of relationships you're having now? Are any of them what you want in a future relationship?

Relationships and Love Edition

Check off each option that you *haven't* experienced.

- ☐ Had a relationship that lasted longer than a year

- ☐ Had a relationship that lasted longer than a few months

- ☐ Been in love

- ☐ Felt loved in a relationship

- ☐ Said "I love you"

- ☐ Said "I love you" *first*

- ☐ Heard a partner say "I love you"

- ☐ Met a partner's parent(s)

- ☐ Introduced a partner to your parent(s)

- ☐ Been engaged

- ☐ Been married

What do you think has held you back from experiencing any "nevers" you have checked off? Are there any you absolutely want to experience in the future? Any you are fine with having as a "never" forever?

Your Best Dating Experiences

Write your answers on the lines provided.

The best date you've ever been on was:

_____

_____

You remember this date because the experience made you feel:

_____

_____

The best person you've dated was:

_____

_____

This person made you feel:

_____

_____

You learned that you needed the following in a relationship:

_____

_____

The downfall of this relationship was:

_____

_____

Things didn't work out, because you and the other person:

_____

_____

This person/experience changed your expectations because:

_____

_____

This person/experience showed you:

_____

_____

Taking these past experiences into account, what goals can you set for the future? Though your best dating experiences—so *far*—may be in your past, you can use them to create standards for relationships to come.

The Craziest Things You've Done for Love

Write your answers on a separate piece of paper.

1. When you were hard-core crushing on someone...

2. When you were so in love...

3. When you felt hurt...

4. When you felt jealous...

5. When you wanted to make someone jealous...

6. When you felt furious...

7. When you felt sad...

8. When you tried to win someone back...

9. When you wanted someone to regret losing you...

10. When you wanted revenge...

Many people have gone a little insane—or thought about it—for someone they loved (or lusted over). Make sure to laugh a little at your crazy-in-love antics and remember that you're human. Things happen; what matters is that you've learned from these experiences.

Toxic Types You've Totally Dated

Check off each option that applies to you, and add your own options to the list on the lines provided.

☐ The people pleaser   ☐ The victim

☐ The critic   ☐ The control freak

☐ The smotherer   ☐ The gossip

☐ The drama queen/king   ☐ The perfectionist

☐ The narcissist   ☐ The overgrown child

☐ The liar   ☐ _____

☐ The cheater   ☐ _____

Recognizing a toxic partner for who they are helps you avoid the same types in the future. (Of course, bad behavior can certainly be changed when a partner is open and willing to improve: This quiz relates to those who simply can't or don't want to work on themselves.) Think about how these people made you feel and what you can do to weed out bad matches in the future. What red flags did you overlook or excuse when dating them?

Your Worst Dating Experiences

Write your answers on the lines provided.

The worst date you've ever been on was:

_____

_____

You remember this date because it made you feel:

_____

_____

The worst person you've dated was:

_____

_____

These experiences taught you:

_____

_____

The most hurtful thing that's ever happened to you while dating was:

_____

_____

You've felt compassion and empathy during a bad date when:

_____

_____

You've felt disheartened on a bad date when:

_____

_____

You've felt like giving up on love when:

_____

_____

You've felt not good enough when:

_____

_____

The best part about your worst dating experiences—besides the fact that they're over—is that they teach you what you definitely *don't* want for your future. Your responses to these questions will inform your present, reminding you to listen to your intuition whenever toxic people or feelings emerge in your dating life.

Your Dating Habits

Circle the option in each question that best applies to you.

1. How would you describe your dating life thus far?
    a. Fun, fast, and furious
    b. Tactical and goal-oriented
    c. Boring

2. If you had had a dating motto when you were younger, what would it have been?
    a. One date at a time
    b. Focus on the big picture
    c. It's all good

3. How aware were you of your wants and needs when you started dating?
    a. Very aware
    b. Sort of aware
    c. Not at all aware

4. How much weight did you give your *wants* when you started dating?
    a. A lot
    b. Some
    c. None

5. How much weight did you give your *needs*?
    a. A lot
    b. Some
    c. None

6. How much do you think you should prioritize your wants versus your needs now?
   a. Wants and needs are equal
   b. Wants are more important
   c. Needs are more important

7. How would you describe your past dating or relationship style?
   a. Serial monogamist
   b. First-date frenzy
   c. All over the place

8. What would you want to say to your former self as you look back on your dating life?
   a. I'm sorry
   b. That was fun
   c. I could have done better

9. How have you evolved in your dating life?
   a. I'm more discerning
   b. I'm more open to possibilities
   c. I'm more straightforward

10. How have you evolved as a partner?
    a. I'm more self-aware
    b. I'm more empathetic
    c. I'm more independent

Use your responses to these questions to think about how your concept of partnership has evolved over time, and what good habits you've developed from your dating experiences. What bad habits do you still want to overcome? What's the most important thing you've learned?

Dating Red Flags You Were Most Likely to Commit

Circle the option in each scenario that resonates most with you.

When it comes to red flags, in the past you...

WOULD: O Show up to a date super-late
O Arrive way too early and get drunk before your date shows up

WOULD: O Talk about yourself the entire time
O Talk about your ex the entire time

WOULD: O Check your phone the entire time
O Watch the game on the TV behind your date the entire time

WOULD: O Bad-mouth your boss   O Brag about your job

WOULD: O Talk rudely to the staff at the bar you're at
O Flirt with the staff

WOULD: O Complain about work the entire time
O Complain about your family the entire time

WOULD: O Pretend to be interested when you aren't
O Play it cool when you are actually feeling it

WOULD: O Itemize the bill   O Make a big show of picking up the tab

It's safe to say that everyone has committed a red flag behavior (or two) over their dating history. But being aware of the things you have done that may turn people off can better help you avoid these behaviors in the future.

How Have the People You've Dated Affected...

Write your answers on a separate piece of paper.

1. Your taste in music?

2. The way you dress?

3. The places you've lived?

4. Your social media habits?

5. The movies you love/hate?

6. The foods you eat?

7. Your personal habits?

8. Your sexual preferences and desires?

9. Your circle of friends?

10. Your relationships with family members?

Sometimes relationships change you in the best of ways, opening up your world to new experiences and rituals you wouldn't otherwise have encountered. They can also be a less-than-ideal influence. It's worth exploring how the person you are today has been shaped by the people you've dated.

What Did Your Friends Think?

Circle the option in each question that best applies to you.

1. How would you describe your friend group through the years?
   a. Primarily the same gender/gender identity as me
   b. Primarily different genders/gender identities than me
   c. An even mix of genders/gender identities

2. In the past, how have your friends encouraged your romantic journey?
   a. They were supportive of my choices
   b. They disapproved of my choices
   c. They had mixed reactions depending on the person I was dating

3. How supportive have your friends been when you've sought love advice in the past?
   a. They were just as clueless as I was
   b. They were superhelpful
   c. They steered me in the wrong direction

4. Have you ever fallen out with a friend because of a dating situation?
   a. Yes, because of someone they've dated
   b. Yes, because of someone I've dated
   c. No

5. Have your friends been hard on the people you've dated in the past?
   a. Yes, because they've tried to protect me
   b. Yes, because they were jealous of my relationship
   c. No, they generally gave the people I've dated a fair chance

6. How much weight have you given your friends' opinions through the years?
   a. A lot...maybe too much
   b. A healthy amount
   c. Not much

7. Have you ever dated someone who you were friends with first?
   a. Never
   b. Yes, and it was great
   c. Yes, and it was a disaster

8. Has a friend ever wanted to date you but you turned them down?
   a. Yes—best decision ever
   b. Yes—and I wish I hadn't
   c. No

9. Have you ever omitted details when telling friends about a relationship because you were worried about their reaction?
   a. Yes—my friends would have scared that person away
   b. Yes, and I wish I had told them the truth so they could have talked me out of a bad situation
   c. No, I've always been up-front with them

10. Why have your friends discouraged you from coupling up with someone in the past?
   a. They wanted me to date someone nicer
   b. They wanted me to date someone who was more like them
   c. They haven't discouraged me

Your social circle can be a powerful influencer in your romantic relationships. Use the results from this quiz to think about how supportive your friends have been in your past and what role you want them to play in your future love story.

Between the Sheets Edition

Check off each option that you *haven't* experienced.

- ☐ Had sex on a first date

- ☐ Waited to get intimate until you felt truly ready

- ☐ Turned down the opportunity for sex

- ☐ Had an orgasm with another person

- ☐ Had sex with someone *without* having an orgasm

- ☐ Told a partner directly what you like in bed

- ☐ Told a partner to stop when you felt physically uncomfortable during sex

- ☐ Zoned out during sex, waiting for it to be over already

- ☐ Spent the night after having sex

- ☐ Left as soon as the sex was over

- ☐ Had makeup sex

- ☐ Had breakup sex

Think of your responses in this quiz as a good jumping-off point for which sexual experiences you wish you'd had (and may want to pursue at some point), which ones you want to keep as "nevers" in a future relationship, and which ones you might've had in the past but never want to have again.

Where Does Sex Factor In?

Write your answers on the lines provided.

Sex has been the _____ part of your past relationships.

The best sex you've ever had was _____ because

_____

The worst sex you've ever had was _____ because

_____

Your biggest sex regret is:

_____

_____

You wish you had waited to have sex when:

_____

_____

You wish you hadn't waited to have sex when:

_____

_____

Sometimes, you've used sex to _____ in past relationships.

You've felt pressured or manipulated into having sex when:

_____

_____

You've withheld sex when you wanted:

_____

_____

You've had sex withheld from you when:

_____

_____

For many people, a healthy sex life is an important part of any romantic relationship. Use the results of this quiz to better understand the role sex has played in your past, and how you want it to play out in relationships moving forward.

Relationship Mistakes You've Made

Check off each option that applies to you, and add your own options to the list on the lines provided.

- ☐ Stayed in a relationship longer than you should have

- ☐ Slept with someone, only to regret it afterward

- ☐ Tried to "fix" or change your partner

- ☐ Dated someone because you liked the *idea* of them/ the relationship

- ☐ Got too comfortable in a relationship—and didn't attempt to get the romance back

- ☐ Expected your partner to be perfect

- ☐ Kept secrets from your partner

- ☐ Didn't take care of yourself (e.g., your mental or physical health)

- ☐ Didn't fully appreciate your partner

- ☐ Turned everything into an argument

- ☐ _____

- ☐ _____

Suffice to say, you probably don't want to repeat the behaviors you've checked off in this quiz. Being honest with yourself about the role you've played in why past unions didn't work out allows you to learn and grow from these mistakes.

Little White Lies Edition

Check off each option that you *haven't* experienced.

☐ Cried to win sympathy from a past partner

☐ Pretended to like a certain band (or movie, workout type, etc.)

☐ Played down the negative aspects of a past relationship or life experience

☐ Lied to protect someone's feelings

☐ Faked an orgasm

☐ Pretended to have a headache to get out of sex (or dinner with their parent/parents)

☐ Said something didn't bother you when it *so* did

☐ Laughed at a joke you didn't find funny

☐ Pretended to get what someone was talking about just so they'd finish the story

Yes, little white lies like these can be fairly harmless—and you'd be hard-pressed to find someone who hasn't told a small lie or two. But if you find after looking back at each option you've left unmarked that you've fallen into a pattern of constantly skirting the truth to save face—or someone's feelings—it's worth paying attention to why you're doing this and what the impact may be over time.

Breakup Experiences You've Likely Had

Circle the option in each scenario that resonates most with you.

In past breakup situations, you...

WOULD: O Let issues fester until a breakup is inevitable
O Talk things out until you realize it's just not going to work

WOULD: O Initiate the breakup
O Get broken up with

WOULD: O Break up for good the first time
O Get back together multiple times before finally calling it quits

WOULD: O Suddenly and dramatically break up
O Experience a breakup that was a long time coming

WOULD: O Act maturely in the aftermath
O Act unreasonably in the aftermath

WOULD: O Blame yourself
O Blame the other person

WOULD: O Vent about your new ex to friends
O Keep issues between the two of you

WOULD: O Go public with the breakup on social media right away
        O Text only your close friends/family about it

WOULD: O Cope by getting back out in the dating scene
        O Cope by taking a break from romance

Think about what usually leads to the end of relationships for you—and what your reactions are to these breakups. What can you learn from the answers to these quiz questions about how you deal with your romantic losses and disappointments?

Feedback from Past Partners

Write your answers on the lines provided.

Your ex(es) would say your best quality is:

_____

_____

Your ex(es) would say your worst quality is:

_____

_____

You still remember an ex telling you that you're:

_____

_____

When you think about the opinion(s) of your ex(es) of you, you feel:

_____

_____

Your ex(es) thought you were too:

_____

_____

When you hear the voice of your ex(es) in your head, they're saying:

_____

_____

The last thing your ex(es) said to you was:

_____

_____

One thing you need to work on, according to your ex(es), is:

_____

_____

One thing you were awesome at, according to your ex(es), was:

_____

_____

Overall, as a partner, your ex(es) would say you're:

_____

_____

The things your exes tell you about yourself can hold a lot of weight—for better or for worse. Which opinions of your ex(es) may be true—and can serve as constructive feedback—and which ones do you now feel you need to let go of for your own sanity?

The Trust Factor

Circle the option in each question that best applies to you.

1. How has trust factored into your past relationships?
   a. It's been a nonissue
   b. It's been a major pain point
   c. It's been a combination of both

2. How important has it been for you to be able to trust your past partners?
   a. It's been essential
   b. It hasn't been superimportant
   c. I've never had a serious relationship, so it's not been a big deal

3. How long does it take for someone to earn your trust?
   a. I trust pretty instantly
   b. It doesn't take superlong
   c. It takes a while

4. How trusting have you been in your past relationships?
   a. Too trusting
   b. Too guarded
   c. The right amount

5. What happens when someone breaks your trust?
   a. I shut down and shut the person out for good
   b. I want to hash out what happened over and over
   c. I need space at first, but I can talk about it eventually

6. If you've broken a partner's trust before, how did you try to earn that trust back?
    a. By going over the top with good behavior
    b. By giving them space
    c. By agreeing to talk it out or go to therapy

7. How did that work for you?
    a. Not so good
    b. It worked for a while—until it didn't
    c. It's complicated: _____ (explain)

8. How have you discussed trust and loyalty with past partners?
    a. I haven't
    b. I discussed it early on—well before making a solid commitment
    c. I discussed it after making it official

9. Can you have a relationship without trust?
    a. Yes
    b. No
    c. It depends: _____ (explain)

Trust is one of the pillars of a strong relationship: Without it, the entire union can crumble. Understanding what trust means to you and how it has manifested in your romantic past can provide insight on what you may need in your connections going forward. What do the results of this quiz tell you about your relationship with trust?

Cheating and Lying Edition

Check off each option that you *haven't* experienced.

☐ Told your partner a lie about your financial or career situation

☐ Hid a physical object in your home so your date/partner wouldn't see it

☐ Cheated on a partner

☐ Been cheated on

☐ Lied to friends about how your relationship was going

☐ Lied to yourself about how your relationship was going

☐ Lied to family about being in a relationship or about your partner

Being honest with yourself—and with others—is critical for success in any relationship. Having your trust broken, or breaking someone else's trust, can affect everything from how you feel about a person, to how your bond with them will develop as time goes on. Use the results of this quiz to examine how lack of honesty has affected your relationships in the past, and what lessons these experiences may hold for you.

How You've Dealt with Negative Experiences in the Past

Circle the option in each scenario that resonates most with you.

During a bad situation, you...

WOULD: O Let it go   O Analyze it to death

WOULD: O Ignore it   O Use it to help you grow

WOULD: O Talk about it   O Keep it all inside

WOULD: O Wallow in your emotions
O Pretend you don't have any emotions

WOULD: O Keep wishing for an apology
O Stop waiting for what may never come

WOULD: O Wait for time to heal your wounds   O Live in the present

WOULD: O Forgive and forget   O Hold on to animosity

WOULD: O Find the lesson   O Feel resentment

WOULD: O Right your past wrongs   O Refuse to swallow your pride

Rather than trying to simply "get over it," use this quiz to get curious about your relationship with past events. How does the way you handled these events affect your emotions today? Which of these emotions might you want to address and possibly heal before entering a romantic relationship in the future?

Holding On to Your Romantic Past

Write your answers on the lines provided.

Your romantic past still affects you by:

_____

_____

The one thing you would change about your romantic past is:

_____

_____

You still carry a grudge toward:

_____

_____

If you could ask an ex anything, you would ask _____ about

_____

If you had the chance, you would apologize to_____for

_____

Being forgiven for a relationship mistake you made would make you feel:

_____

_____

You're still bitter about:

_____

_____

You still beat yourself up over:

_____

_____

You still wonder "what if" about:

_____

_____

You still need to forgive yourself for:

_____

_____

If you were to really let go of your romantic past and focus on the **present**, you would feel: _____

_____

Past relationships can be tough to overcome. No matter how over it you may feel you are, you may still have nagging questions about what happened, or wish you had a time machine so you could change history. Getting it all out in this quiz can help you transcend some of these feelings and move on for good.

Do You Agree That...

Circle the option in each question that best applies to you.

1. **You've gained useful insight from your past dating experiences?**
   a. Agree
   b. Disagree
   c. It's complicated: _____ (explain)

2. **You've healed from your past relationships?**
   a. Agree
   b. Disagree
   c. It's complicated: _____ (explain)

3. **Looking back, you now believe that you've dated certain people for a specific reason?**
   a. Agree
   b. Disagree
   c. It's complicated: _____ (explain)

4. **None of your past relationships were mistakes?**
   a. Agree
   b. Disagree
   c. It's complicated: _____ (explain)

5. **You've grown as a person and a partner since you started dating?**
   a. Agree
   b. Disagree
   c. It's complicated: _____ (explain)

6. You can take responsibility for your past relationship mistakes?
   a. Agree
   b. Disagree
   c. It's complicated: _____ (explain)

7. Your outlook on love has shifted over time for the better?
   a. Agree
   b. Disagree
   c. It's complicated: _____ (explain)

8. Your relationship baggage will be useful in future relationships?
   a. Agree
   b. Disagree
   c. It's complicated: _____ (explain)

9. It would be worthwhile to share your past experiences with a future partner?
   a. Agree
   b. Disagree
   c. It's complicated: _____ (explain)

10. You're ready to let go of your romantic past and focus on the future?
   a. Agree
   b. Disagree
   c. It's complicated: _____ (explain)

Your romantic past is a useful tool for outlining what works for you, what doesn't work for you, and where you want to ultimately end up in terms of future attachments. Use this holistic view of your experiences to inspire your journey of self-inquiry and help you become the best person— and partner—you can be.

Who You've Been in Past Relationships

Write your answers on a separate piece of paper.

1. How would you describe the person (or different people) you have been in past relationships (e.g., adventurous, suspicious, fashionable)?

2. What do you like about the person (or different people) you were?

3. What don't you like about the person (or different people) you were?

4. How well did you maintain your sense of self in past relationships?

5. In what ways have you been consumed by past relationships?

6. How have you changed following these relationships?

7. How have people you've dated tried to change you or encouraged you to change?

8. How have you let them change you?

9. What kind of feedback have you received from people you love and trust about who you were while in a relationship?

10. What have you learned about who you are, or who you become, when you're in a relationship?

11. How has a fear of breaking up or of being alone possibly encouraged you to stay in a relationship for longer than you should have?

Use this quiz to delve deep into your past relationships. What type of person have these relationships compelled you to be? Through this exploration into your past, you can learn how you might become more in tune with how your relationships affect you, so you can be the best possible partner to that future special someone.

Part 2

PRESENT

Now that you've taken a closer look at where you've been, it's time to check in with where you are now. A major part of finding the best partner for you is being the best possible version of *yourself*. Of course, that doesn't mean changing who you are in order to win someone over: It means being the most *you* that you possibly can be. When you understand yourself inside and out, you do the things that make you feel the happiest and most fulfilled. And you avoid the stuff that just isn't working for you. Therefore, when you understand what you really want and need, you are better equipped to evaluate potential partners for the kind of person who would truly complement you, instead of settling for whoever slides into your DMs.

With this in mind, the quizzes in this section are here to help you not only to get real with yourself, but also to discover how you can better cherish and appreciate who you are. After all, if you can't love yourself, how are you going to love someone else?

You Are...

Check off each option that applies to you, and add your own options to the list on the lines provided.

☐ A loyal friend   ☐ A respectful person

☐ A good listener   ☐ A reliable person

☐ An intelligent person   ☐ A generous person

☐ A supportive person   ☐ An amusing person

☐ A loving friend   ☐ _____

☐ An empathetic person   ☐ _____

☐ A genuine person

Quick: Go put these terms on your dating profile, *stat*. Seriously though, it's important to know the awesome qualities you bring to the dating table. Use this quiz to remember what a catch you are the next time you're feeling disappointed by a bad date or fizzled text conversation.

Who You Are in One Word According to...

Write your answers on the lines provided.

Your parent(s):

_____

_____

Your grandparent(s):

_____

Your sibling(s):

_____

_____

Your best friend: _____

Your boss: _____

Your work BFF: _____

Your employee: _____

Your neighbor: _____

Your former/current roommate:

_____

Your favorite teacher:

_____

    The people closest to you likely have a different view of who you are than you do. After all, they see you without the filter of your own inner monologue, which can often be self-critical. Feel free to give your own guesses for the people listed, then ask them for their responses. You may be surprised by their answers—and the difference to your own guesses.

Your Core Values

Write your answers on a separate piece of paper.

1. What values are most important to you in all areas of your life (e.g., family, love, career)?

2. What actions are you currently taking that support these values?

3. How does your current career support your values?

4. How do your values play into your different family and friend relationships?

5. How do your values influence your daily decision-making?

6. Is there any part of your current life that's at odds with your values?

7. How did you decide on your values?

8. When was a time that you strayed from one or more of your values?

9. How did you get back on track?

Your core values are the standards that you live your life by. If you compromise on your values, or push them aside, you immediately feel that things aren't right—and it affects your overall happiness. A potential ideal partner will share these values (or at least appreciate them), and will not push you to change or ignore your positive beliefs.

How You Describe Yourself

Circle the option in each scenario that resonates most with you.

You...

ARE: O Optimistic O Pessimistic

ARE: O Logical O Emotional

ARE: O Book-smart O Street-smart

ARE: O Anxious O Easygoing

ARE: O Impulsive O Calculated

ARE: O Adventurous O Cautious

ARE: O Moody O Chill

ARE: O Gullible O Skeptical

ARE: O Cat-loving O Dog-loving

ARE: O Go-getting O Go-with-the-flow

ARE: O Passionate O Coolheaded

Looking at your selections, how important is it to you that your future partner share these same traits? How might someone with the opposite qualities balance you out, or challenge you in either good or bad ways?

Loving Yourself

Write your answers on the lines provided.

You'd describe your current level of self-esteem as:

_____

_____

Your self-esteem is most influenced by:

_____

_____

Your confidence level used to be _____,
and now it's _____

You feel most confident when you're:

_____

_____

You feel least confident when you're:

_____

_____

You're way too hard on yourself about:

_____

_____

Your confidence is often rattled by:

_____

_____

The habits, people, or situations that make you feel good about yourself are:

_____

_____

The habits, people, or situations that make you feel not-so-good about yourself are: _____

_____

Being in a relationship affects your self-esteem by:

_____

_____

Your sense of self affects your ability not only to accept love, but also to give it. Use this quiz to check in with your confidence level and see if you need to give a little extra nurturing to the most important relationship you'll ever have: the one with yourself.

Your Self-Destruct Buttons

Check off each option that applies to you, and add your own options to the list on the lines provided.

☐ Fear of abandonment

☐ Body issues

☐ People-pleasing tendencies

☐ The struggle to find true purpose

☐ Unreliability

☐ Addictive personality

☐ Feelings of not being "enough"

☐ The belief that your problems are always someone else's fault

☐ Lack of boundaries

☐ Fear of being alone

☐ Unhealthy lifestyle

☐ _____

☐ _____

It's safe to say that the items you checked off are worth some extra attention now—not only so you can find a forever partnership, but also so you can be the best version of yourself possible, for *you*.

How Much Pressure Do You Put on Yourself to...

Circle the option in each question that best applies to you.

1. Excel at work?
   a. A lot
   b. Some
   c. None

2. Own your own home?
   a. A lot
   b. Some
   c. None

3. Find love?
   a. A lot
   b. Some
   c. None

4. Maintain a photo-worthy living space?
   a. A lot
   b. Some
   c. None

5. Make your life look good on social media?
   a. A lot
   b. Some
   c. None

6. Be a good friend?
   a. A lot
   b. Some
   c. None

7. Call your parent(s)?
   a. A lot
   b. Some
   c. None

8. Work out?
   a. A lot
   b. Some
   c. None

9. Eat right?

    a.   A lot

    b.   Some

    c.   None

10. Look a certain way?

    a.   A lot

    b.   Some

    c.   None

11. Act morally?

    a.   A lot

    b.   Some

    c.   None

12. Be liked by others?

    a.   A lot

    b.   Some

    c.   None

The (sometimes unrealistic) expectations you have for your life can often get projected onto a prospective romantic partner. You may expect the people you meet to excel in the areas you feel you're underachieving in—or in areas you are also excelling in—or you may be more sensitive to criticism from people in these areas. Knowing what issues trigger certain expectations or assumptions in yourself can help you understand what may turn you off to some people or draw you toward others.

Worry about:

Check off each option that applies to you.

- [ ] Ending up with the wrong person

- [ ] Being the last one among your friends to get married/commit to a relationship

- [ ] Missing out on:

    _____

- [ ] Working too much

- [ ] Lacking dating experience

- [ ] Lacking sexual experience

- [ ] Having too much sexual experience

- [ ] Waiting too long to have kids

- [ ] Failing at being an adult

- [ ] Being an "imposter"

- [ ] Not being able to provide for a family

- [ ] Not being able to get out of debt

- [ ] Making the wrong decision about:

    _____

What you worry about can keep you up at night—and hold you back from living an honest, vibrant life. Use your responses to this quiz as a starting point for turning any current worries into acceptance for the things you can't change and actions for the things you can.

Spirituality and the Universe's Plan

Write your answers on the lines provided.

The role religion plays in your current life is:

_____

_____

You used to feel_____

about religion and now you feel_____

_____

The role spirituality plays in your life is:

_____

_____

A benefit of believing/not believing in a higher power is:

_____

_____

You believe/don't believe that your life is outside of your control, because:

_____

_____

When you think about an outside force directing your life, you feel:

_____

_____

You believe/don't believe that a higher power has a plan for you, because:

_____

_____

You believe/don't believe that everything happens for a reason, because:

_____

_____

You believe that religion will play_____

role in your future relationships.

You want your future partner to feel_____

about religion/spirituality.

Your views about religion/spirituality may shape your worldview *and* have a significant impact on future relationships. Is it important to you that your future partner share your spiritual or religious outlook?

Your Current Family Relationships

Write your answers on a separate piece of paper.

1. How close are you to your family members?

2. In what ways are you close with them?

3. In what ways are you not close with them?

4. Which family member(s) do you feel closest with, and what makes those relationships special?

5. Which family member(s) do you have a tough relationship with, and what makes those relationships strained?

6. How would you describe your current relationship with your parent(s)?

7. How do your current parental relationships shape your views of partnership and family?

8. In what ways might you be seeking out partners who are similar to your parent(s)?

9. In what ways might you be avoiding partners who are similar to your parent(s)?

10. How important is it to you that your family supports your choice in partner?

11. What kind of pressure has your family put on you to find a partner?

12. What kind of partner does your family want you to choose?

Your family relationships not only have shaped the person that you are today, but also continue to affect the way you relate to others, especially romantic partners. Use your responses to these questions to explore the ways your unique family situation may influence your future love life.

Your Current Relationship with Your Parents

Circle the option in each scenario that resonates most with you.

You...

ARE: O Close to them
O Politely civil (or not close at all)

TALK: O Every day
O Every month (or less)

STAY: O With them when you visit
O At a hotel

FEEL: O Able to talk to them about everything
O Like you have to hide key parts of your life

FEEL: O Like they can relate to you
O Like you're generations apart

FEEL: O Accepted by them
O Judged by them

TALK: O As equals
O As a child and a parent

WOULD: O Ask them for advice
         O Never seek their counsel

WOULD: O Openly share negative feedback with them
         O Never share constructive criticism with them

WANT: O A similar relationship with your own future kids
         O A different dynamic

Your relationships with your parents may be the longest lasting of your life. From the day you were born, they have likely shaped your wants, needs, and beliefs throughout the years. So it makes sense that the dynamic you have with them will impact your love life now and in the future, especially if you have—or intend to someday have—a family of your own.

Understanding
Your Attachment Style

Write your answers on the lines provided.

You feel _____ when someone you love

tries to take care of you.

When someone you love is unpredictable (e.g., calling consistently one

day and then silent the next), you feel:_____

_____

When you can count on someone in your life no matter what, you feel:

_____

_____

When things are going well for you in life, you often feel:

_____

_____

When you fight with people you love, you worry that:

_____

_____

The most uncomfortable thing about being in conflict with other people is:

_____

_____

You've felt afraid of getting too close to someone (either a friend or someone you're dating) when: _____

_____

One thing that sometimes gets in the way of you giving and/or receiving love is:

_____

_____

You feel safe and comfortable in your relationships when:

_____

_____

You focus on meeting other people's needs over your own when:

_____

_____

Your attachment style (secure attachment, anxious preoccupied attachment, dismissive avoidant attachment, or fearful avoidant attachment) can affect all of your relationships, but most significantly the ones you have with romantic partners. A dismissive avoidant attachment style, for example, can lead to unfounded trust issues or constant questioning of a relationship. Using your answers to these questions, look at the descriptions of each attachment style online to find out your own style. Figuring out your attachment style will help you uncover what draws you to certain types of partners, and whether there may be underlying insecurities or unhealthy behaviors to address.

Your Life Is Together(ish) Because You...

Check off each option that applies to you, and add your own options to the list on the lines provided.

☐ Have a good credit score

☐ Pay your bills

☐ Pay your taxes

☐ Take care of yourself physically and mentally

☐ Regularly see the doctor

☐ Generally arrive on time to things

☐ Are totally capable of pet-sitting for someone

☐ Offer to be the designated driver

☐ Call your friends back

☐ Call your parent(s) back

☐ Know how to cook at least a few solid meals

☐ Know how to do your own laundry

- [ ] Feel proud of where you live

- [ ] Feel like you can make your own decisions

- [ ] Ask for help when you need it

- [ ] Almost never misplace your credit card, wallet, keys, or other essentials

- [ ] Clean your fridge and toss out expired food regularly

- [ ] Almost never wear pajamas in public

- [ ] _____

- [ ] _____

You don't need to have your *whole* life together to find a lasting relationship, but it definitely doesn't hurt to get yourself to a good place before you begin giving more of your time and attention to a partner. How many of the unchecked things in this list do you still want to accomplish before meeting that special someone?

How's That Temper?

Circle the option in each question that best applies to you.

1. How do you feel when you're fighting with someone you love?
   a. Stressed
   b. Angry
   c. Sad

2. How much do you enjoy being right or "winning" an argument?
   a. A lot
   b. A little
   c. I don't need to be right; I just want the fight to end

3. Who in your life pushes your buttons the most?
   a. My parent(s)
   b. My boss
   c. My friends
   d. Someone else:_____(who?)

4. Why do you think you and this person/these people tend to butt heads?
   a. We're very similar
   b. We're very different
   c. Something else: _____ (what?)

5. How heated do you get when in the midst of an argument?
   a. I get very heated
   b. I'm able to stay levelheaded for the most part
   c. I tend to cry more than yell

6. How hurt do you feel when you're in the middle of a conflict?
   a. Like, a lot
   b. More anxious than hurt
   c. More angry than hurt

7. How quick are you to anger?
    a. It doesn't take much
    b. It takes something major
    c. It depends: _____ (explain)

8. How long does it take for you to get over a conflict or argument?
    a. A long time
    b. Not long
    c. As soon as the other person apologizes

9. How easy is it for you to forgive?
    a. Very easy
    b. Somewhat easy
    c. Not very easy

10. Has your way of fighting/resolving conflict done more to help or hurt your relationships?
    a. Help
    b. Hurt
    c. It's less clear-cut: _____(explain)

11. What do you wish you could change or work on in regards to your fighting style?
    a. I want to be more forgiving
    b. I want to stand up for myself more
    c. Something else: _____ (explain)

All couples fight, no matter how happy they are together. Determining the degree to which your own fighting style is fair and effective can help you make future conflicts with a partner as productive and loving as possible.

How You Resolve Conflict

Circle the option in each scenario that resonates most with you.

When there is an issue, you...

WILL: O Talk about it in person
O Talk over text

WILL: O Speak up right away about something that bothers you
O Let it fester

WILL: O Admit when you're wrong
O Make excuses

WILL: O Interrupt so you can have your say
O Remain quiet while the other person talks

WILL: O Play the blame game
O Overapologize

WILL: O Cry   O Yell

WILL: O Use absolutes ("you always," "I never")
O Focus on the specific issue at hand

WILL: O Ask exploratory questions ("How can we solve this?")
O Ask accusatory questions ("Why are you like this?")

WILL: O Acknowledge the other person's feelings
        O Focus on your side of things

WILL: O Apologize first
        O Wait for the other person to

WILL: O Hug it out
        O Prefer to not be touched for a while

How you resolve an argument can be just as revealing as how you start or engage in one. Use your choices circled to evaluate your relationship with conflict and the reasons you react the way you do. How might you evolve these behaviors going forward to make arguments with a partner as constructive as possible?

Face Value

Write your answers on the lines provided.

You feel most attractive when:

_____

_____

Your favorite body part is your:

_____

_____

Your least favorite body part is your:

_____

_____

To other people, the most physically attractive things about you are:

_____

_____

You spend _____ (amount of time) thinking about the way you look.

You spend _____ (amount of time) trying to improve the way you look.

Your relationship with the way you look has affected:

_____

_____

If you could change anything about how you look, it would be:

_____

_____

When you look in the mirror, you usually feel:

_____

_____

When you look at old pictures of yourself, you feel:

_____

_____

Apart from the obvious importance of self-love, feeling good about yourself translates to feeling good in other aspects of your life, including your relationships with others. So how comfortable are you in your own skin? What things do you want to someday feel better about?

Judge People for:

Check off each option that applies to you.

- ☐ Having bad skin
- ☐ Having "bad" taste in music/movies/pop culture
- ☐ Displaying a lack of eloquence
- ☐ Having clothes that don't fit/look right
- ☐ Being in debt
- ☐ Being "basic"
- ☐ Being picky eaters

- ☐ Not being "woke" enough
- ☐ Posting food pictures on *Instagram*
- ☐ Drinking/not drinking alcohol
- ☐ Doing/not doing drugs
- ☐ Living with a roommate
- ☐ Living with their parent(s)
- ☐ Trying "too hard"

Even the kindest, most open-minded people judge others from time to time. However, it's important to be aware of what you do judge others for, and whether these judgments are fair. You wouldn't want to write off a potential partner for something that you may later feel doesn't matter.

Career Aspirations and Priorities

Circle the option in each question that best applies to you.

1. To what extent does your career define you?
    a. A lot—I'm proud of what I do and it's the most significant thing about me
    b. Some—I like my job but I'm not married to it
    c. Not at all

2. How much have you prioritized your career in your life so far?
    a. My career comes first
    b. My career is important but it's not the number one thing
    c. Career? More like a job—clock in, clock out

3. How much do you want to prioritize your career going forward?
    a. I'm happy with how I prioritize it now
    b. I could take things down a notch
    c. I need to be more serious about it

4. Do you want to be the sole/main earner in your future partnership?
    a. Yes
    b. No
    c. It depends: _____ (explain)

5. How would you feel if you suddenly lost your job?
    a. I'd be devastated
    b. I'd be upset but I'd bounce back quickly
    c. I'd miss the paycheck but that's about it

6. What does a potential partner need to know about your career aspirations?
   a. That I'm kind of a workaholic
   b. That I'm good at what I do but it's not my identity
   c. That I'm probably never going to have a corner office

7. Do you think your career has held you back romantically?
   a. Yes—I've put having a serious relationship on the back burner
   b. Somewhat, especially when I've needed to focus on big projects
   c. Not at all

8. What may need to change about your commitment to your career in order for you to have a committed relationship?
   a. I need to find more balance
   b. My career isn't the issue
   c. I should probably focus more on my career

9. How would you feel about having a relationship with someone in the same career field as you?
   a. Totally cool
   b. Wouldn't matter
   c. Totally not cool

10. How likely is it that you would be a stay-at-home parent?
    a. It is out of the question
    b. It's possible
    c. I'd love to

Your answers to this quiz can shed light on your current relationship with your career, and the ways that relationship may be affecting your love life.

Your Accomplishments

Check off each option that applies to you, and add your own options to the list on the lines provided.

- ☐ An awesome group of friends

- ☐ A healthy relationship with your parents (or a thankfully nonexistent relationship)

- ☐ A steady job

- ☐ Financial stability (or on the right track to finding it)

- ☐ A hobby (or hobbies) you love

- ☐ A strong sense of self

- ☐ A loyal companion (pet)

- ☐ The ability to speak in more than one language

- ☐ A conquered fear

- ☐ Experiences outside of your home country

- ☐ Your very own living space

- ☐ _____

- ☐ _____

Even if you're still working things out in the romance department, don't forget there's a lot to be proud of about yourself and your life! Focusing on what makes your life full right now will not only promote happiness, but send out those positive vibes to potential partners. They're sure to want in on those good feelings.

What Inspires You?

Write your answers on a separate piece of paper.

1. Do you have a favorite quote or phrase that you live by?

2. Who in your life inspires you?

3. Which current public or historical figures inspire you?

4. How motivated do you feel currently?

5. What drives you?

6. What sets you back or stops you from feeling motivated?

7. In what ways do you want to inspire others?

8. In what areas of your life are you most ambitious?

9. In what areas of your life are you least motivated?

10. What do you think your purpose is in life?

Part of being in a relationship is lifting each other up and helping each other feel inspired. In the present, staying committed to what motivates you not only makes you more attractive to other people, but also gives you a solid sense of self. Hold on to these motivators as you look for compatible partners.

Your Single Life

Write your answers on the lines provided.

You love _____
_____ about being single.

The most frustrating thing about being single is:

_____

_____

You feel disappointed about being single when:

_____

_____

You feel grateful that you're single when:

_____

_____

The best lesson that being single has taught you is:

_____

_____

You'd rather be single than:

_____

_____

The biggest misconception about being single is:

_____

_____

When you find a prospective match, the first thing you think is usually:

_____

_____

After a lackluster date, the voice in your head usually says:

_____

_____

You feel _____ when someone doesn't message you back about getting together IRL.

Being single has its ups and downs, to say the least. Use your responses to these questions to take stock of where you're at right now—and also celebrate what you love about "me time." How might you fit some of these personal wants into a shared life with someone else?

Your Typical Date

Circle the option in each scenario that resonates most with you.

You usually date someone who...

IS:
- O (you feel) More attractive than you
- O (you feel) Less attractive than you

IS:
- O (you feel) Smarter than you
- O (you feel) Less smart than you

HAS:
- O A more easygoing family
- O A more "challenging" family

HAS:
- O Lots of friends
- O A few close friends

IS:
- O A lot like you
- O The total opposite of you

NEEDS:
- O A lot of your attention
- O A lot of independence

IS:
- O Athletic
- O Bookish

IS:
- O Passionate
- O Mellow

IS: O All about you
           O Into being chased

IS: O Loved by your friends
           O Not well-liked by your friends

Knowing who you are typically drawn to opens the door to understanding what qualities are truly important in a relationship, and which ones may be trivial—or even a hindrance in long-term success. Where have the traits you circled played into your love connections? What was good about these traits? What was not so great about them?

Exploring Your Type

Write your answers on a separate piece of paper.

1. What physical qualities do you gravitate toward currently (e.g., tall and mysterious)?

2. What emotional qualities do you gravitate toward currently (e.g., communicative, affectionate)?

3. What lifestyle qualities do you gravitate toward currently (e.g., steady job, outdoorsy type)?

4. Which negative traits may initially attract you to someone (e.g., the enigma, the person in need of saving)?

5. Would people in your life say you have a distinct "type"? If so, what do they say it is?

6. How do you think the people you date reflect who you are or what you believe about yourself?

7. How open are you presently to people who fall outside of your "type"?

Your results here will help you determine what your current "type" (or "types") may be—that is, the people you are most attracted to. From there, you can discover how that attraction stacks up to the things you need in a relationship. How have these type of qualities worked out in your love connections so far?

Feel Attracted:

Check off each option that applies to you.

☐ To someone at first sight

☐ To someone just by hearing their voice

☐ To someone's smell

☐ To someone who is the opposite of you

☐ To someone who you feel is out of your league

☐ To someone who is kind of rude to you

☐ To someone physically but not emotionally

☐ To someone emotionally but not physically

☐ To someone after getting to know them better

Use your selections to reveal the extent to which you believe in the power of physical chemistry. Have you ever felt the urge to stop dating someone after that initial spark wore off? Or, on the flip side, do you often build up to a loving relationship slowly? Factor in these experiences moving forward.

Your Dating Style

Circle the option in each scenario that resonates most with you.

When it comes to dating, you...

ARE:
- O Too picky
- O Not picky enough

WILL:
- O Make the first move
- O Wait to be approached

ARE:
- O Drawn to a good pickup line
- O Turned off by cheesiness

WANT:
- O To be pursued
- O To be the one who chases

PREFER:
- O Long-distance relationships
- O Being in the same city

SPEND:
- O More time texting
- O More time talking face-to-face

PREFER:
- O To get to know someone first virtually
- O To go on an IRL date right away

CHOOSE:
- O A date based on what your head thinks
- O A date based on what your heart feels

TEND: o To end things based on your gut
              o To end a relationship based on the facts of what has happened

TEND: o To analyze everything
              o To just let things unfold as they may

You may know your dating style well at this point, but it's worth looking at the specifics again. How have your dating habits been working—or not working—for you so far? What might you consider changing now to improve them?

Your Relationship Philosophies

Write your answers on a separate piece of paper.

1. What do you feel is the purpose of being in a romantic relationship?

2. How does your current view of relationships differ from past views?

3. What might a romantic relationship add to your life?

4. In what ways might being in a relationship limit you? How do you feel about these limitations?

5. Do you want to find a partner for life, or are you open to casual dates and different partners in the future?

6. Do you believe in the institution of marriage? Why, or why not?

7. How realistic do you believe it is to expect to be with one person for the rest of your life?

8. How long do you think two people should date before committing to marriage?

9. At what point should a couple call it quits?

Knowing your current core beliefs about partnership can help you better choose the right person for you. How important is it that a partner share these views? Come back to these responses often to check in with your relationship goals; things can change over the course of your experiences.

What Things Impact Your Romantic Decisions?

Check off each option that applies to you, and add your own options to the list on the lines provided.

☐ Pressure/expectations from family

☐ Encouragement/discouragement from friends

☐ Desire to be in a certain place in your life by a certain age

☐ Fear of being alone

☐ Fear of breaking up

☐ Fear of ending up with the wrong person

☐ Desire to make a current relationship work

☐ Contentment with settling for "good enough"

☐ Determination *not* to settle for "good enough"

☐ Feeling of being smothered

☐ Craving for love and affection

☐ Feeling of obligation, what you "should" do

☐ _____

☐ _____

In what ways have the factors you checked off affected your romantic relationships—both in the past, and more recently? Think about how much weight you want these things to hold in future connections.

Work On Yourself by:

Check off each option that applies to you.

- ☐ Exercising regularly

- ☐ Practicing positive self-talk

- ☐ Meditating

- ☐ Taking regular time for self-care

- ☐ Going to a therapist

- ☐ Reading self-help books

- ☐ Taking classes to boost your career or nurture your passions

- ☐ Writing in a journal

- ☐ Making a vision board

- ☐ Trying things that are out of your comfort zone

- ☐ Taking steps toward kicking a bad habit

- ☐ Writing to-do lists

- ☐ Cutting negativity out of your life

☐ Working with a mentor

☐ Learning new skills, or exploring topics unfamiliar to you

☐ Practicing gratitude

You are constantly evolving (it's only human!). And this development should ideally continue through your whole life, with or without a partner. Use the methods that have worked—and seek out new ways to improve— to continue growing into the best person (and partner) that you can be.

Your Life Plan

Circle the option in each question that best applies to you.

1. To what extent have you tried to plan out your life thus far?
   a. I'm a planner—period
   b. I like to have a loose plan
   c. I rarely plan anything

2. How's this strategy working for you overall?
   a. Great
   b. Okay
   c. Not great

3. What's the value of having a life plan?
   a. It helps me prioritize
   b. It helps me stay on track
   c. It helps me stave off regret

4. What's the downside of having a life plan?
   a. It makes me feel anxious
   b. It keeps me from living in the present
   c. It doesn't leave room for unexpected opportunities

5. What area of your life is going the best?
   a. Career
   b. Friends and/or family relationships
   c. Other: _____

6. What area of your life is going the worst—or just not as well as you may have hoped?
   a. Career
   b. Friends and/or family relationships
   c. Other: _____

7. How do you feel about being surprised by where life takes you?
   a. Life's a journey and I'm along for the ride
   b. I don't mind a little unexpected excitement every now and then
   c. I just want everything to go as planned

8. How does a long-term relationship fit into your current life plan?
   a. It's the most important thing
   b. It's a priority
   c. It's not as important as other aspects

9. How much do you expect your life to change in the next five years?
   a. A lot
   b. A little
   c. Not much

10. How much do you expect your life to change in the next ten years?
    a. A lot
    b. A little
    c. Not much

The funniest thing about having a life plan is that life often doesn't go as planned. And yet, it's still important to do at least a little prep work to get where you want to go. Use your responses to this quiz to help gauge whether you need a better plan to get back on track with your goals, or if you need to allow for more fluidity to enjoy life's surprises. Once you feel solid with your own road map, you'll be better able to find the right person to join you for the ride.

The Real You

Write your answers on a separate piece of paper.

1. To what extent do you feel there are different versions of you, depending on a given situation or the people you're surrounded by?

2. When do you feel most yourself?

3. Who do you feel sees the *real* you?

4. Who else would you be willing to let in to see the real you?

5. How would you describe your typical emotional state?

6. Is there anything about you that you feel the people in your life wouldn't accept or like if they knew? If so, what?

7. What insecurities may be holding you back from always being yourself?

8. What makes you feel anxious?

9. How might you change your life plan if you knew for certain that you would succeed?

10. What might you do differently if you knew that you wouldn't be judged by others for it?

Many people put up some kind of wall (or even a fortress) to protect their true selves for fear of being judged. But to be in a fulfilling relationship, you need to let your partner know the real you.

Your Social Style

Circle the option in each scenario that resonates most with you.
You...

ARE: O An introvert   O An extrovert

PREFER: O Any opportunity for the *'gram*
        O Being a social media abstainer

PREFER: O A cleverly crafted tweet   O An awesome photo posted

HAVE: O FOMO (fear of missing out)
        O JOMO (joy of missing out)

ARE: O A confident person in social settings
        O Nervous around people you don't know well

PREFER: O To smile and strike up a conversation
        O To avoid eye contact until they speak first

ARE: O An oversharer   O An undersharer

HAVE: O One BFF   O Many close friends

HAVE: O One core group of friends   O Multiple friend groups

ARE: O An open book (let people in right away)
        O A closed book (take a while to let them really know you)

Your responses indicate how you relate to others. Consider your social style: How social do you want your partner to be? How social would you like to be as a couple?

How Your Friends Support Your Love Life (or Don't)

Write your answers on the lines provided.

Of all your friends, you trust _____ the most when it comes to advice about romance and relationships.

Of all your friends, you trust _____ the least when it comes to advice about romance and relationships.

The couple in your life you most admire is_____ because _____

Your friends currently support you in finding a partner by:

_____

_____

Your friends hold you back from finding a partner by:

_____

_____

You wish your friends knew or better understood_____

_____

about your love life.

If your friends offered to set you up, you would say _____
because _____

Your friends think you deserve a romantic partner who:

_____

_____

Your friends encourage you to not make dating or relationship mistakes like:

_____

_____

If you don't find a romantic partner, you might consider marrying

_____ from your friend group.

Your friends can often be an influential force when it comes to finding and settling down with a companion. Maybe they encourage a date you may have otherwise turned down, or maybe they tend to speak negatively about relationships, making you feel more negative about partnerships too. How are *your* friends currently supporting you in this quest for love?

Your Communication Style

Circle the option in each question that best applies to you.

1. How direct are you when communicating with others?
   a. Very
   b. Somewhat
   c. Not at all

2. How often do you keep feelings inside without expressing them to others?
   a. Usually
   b. Sometimes
   c. Never

3. How often do you get frustrated easily when dealing with others?
   a. Usually
   b. Sometimes
   c. Never

4. Have other people labeled you as intimidating (or would you consider yourself intimidating)?
   a. Yes
   b. In certain situations
   c. Never

5. How often do you use sarcasm in conversation?
   a. Usually
   b. Sometimes
   c. Never

6. Do you ever find yourself muttering things under your breath instead of voicing them loud enough for others to hear?
   a. Usually
   b. Sometimes
   c. Never

7. How comfortable are you with clearly stating your opinions?
   a. Very
   b. Somewhat
   c. Not at all

8. How confident do you feel about having a conversation when conflict arises?
   a. Very
   b. Somewhat
   c. Not at all

9. How well can you listen to someone without interrupting?
   a. I listen perfectly
   b. I'm pretty good
   c. I need some work

10. Do you typically make eye contact when you're speaking with someone face-to-face?
    a. Usually
    b. Sometimes
    c. Never

11. Which statement best describes your inner monologue when you communicate with others?
    a. "We are both entitled to our opinions"
    b. "I'll get my way eventually"
    c. "People never consider my feelings"

Knowing how you communicate is crucial for navigating all parts of a romantic relationship, from that very first conversation, to the endless days and nights you'll spend talking with your partner. Is your communication style more passive or more assertive? Are there any areas where you could improve to make your overall communication style as effective as possible for both you and the other people involved?

Your Emotional Triggers

Check off each option that applies to you, and add your own options to the list on the lines provided.

☐ A lot happening at once

☐ Rejection

☐ A mistake you made

☐ Something you did that you feel was embarrassing

☐ Lack of control

☐ An awkward/uncomfortable social situation

☐ The feeling like you are just one of many

☐ Lack of respect by others

☐ An irritating situation

☐ A sad situation

☐ A sense of urgency to a task or decision

☐ Lack of sleep

☐ _____

☐ _____

Knowing what makes you react—whether it's with anger, sadness, etc.—is an important tool, not only for your everyday life, but also for maintaining a healthy relationship. When you can clearly define your triggers, you can better manage emotions so they are less likely to get the best of you.

Feel Regret over:

Check off each option that applies to you.

- ☐ Staying in a relationship for too long

- ☐ Staying in a job position for too long

- ☐ Not taking care of your physical health

- ☐ Not taking care of your mental health

- ☐ Losing touch with friends or loved ones

- ☐ Indulging in too much screen time

- ☐ Portraying your life on social media a certain way

- ☐ Spending too much money

- ☐ Not traveling more

- ☐ Not appreciating yourself more

- ☐ Taking life too seriously

- ☐ Not taking life seriously enough

Aspects of your life that you regret or wish you could change can often manifest in hang-ups or insecurities later on. Find acceptance where you can, and explore ways that you might improve on things you checked off moving forward.

Your Relationship with Money

Write your answers on a separate piece of paper.

1. How would you describe your current relationship with money?

2. What are your most responsible financial habits?

3. What are your least responsible financial habits?

4. How do you deal with any debt you may have?

5. How do you handle any unexpected cash windfalls, like monetary gifts or work bonuses?

6. How have money matters been handled in your family? Are they still handled this way?

7. What scares you the most about your finances?

8. What would it take for you to feel totally financially secure?

9. How would you feel about relying on a partner for financial security?

10. How truthful are you willing to be with a partner about your current financial situation? Why might you hesitate?

Money is one of the biggest issues that couples fight about—and for good reason. Like it or not, money is what allows life to happen, from buying a home and going on vacation, to paying off loans and saving for retirement. How you handle money and how honest you are with yourself and your partner about your financial situation will matter a lot. Use the results of this quiz to examine your own current relationship with money.

Your Financial Goals

Check off each option that applies to you, and add your own options to the list on the lines provided.

☐ Pay off your student loans

☐ Pay off your car

☐ Buy a house

☐ Start a company for yourself/reach a certain pay grade

☐ Save up an emergency fund

☐ Learn how to invest/become more skilled at investing

☐ Save for retirement

☐ Retire before age sixty

☐ Invest in property

☐ Shop at an upscale food market without having to check prices

☐ Take care of your parent(s) when/if they become unable to fully care for themselves

☐ Pay for your kids' college

☐   Regularly contribute to your favorite cause or charity

☐   _____

☐   _____

Knowing what money milestones you want to accomplish in the future will allow you to not only stay on track once there is someone else in the picture, but also communicate your financial priorities to that partner.

Pets and Partners

Circle the option in each question that best applies to you.

1. How important is having a pet to you?
   a. It is very important
   b. I never want a pet
   c. I'd consider it/It is somewhat important

2. If you would never consider having a pet, why not?
   a. I travel (or want to travel) a lot
   b. I'm not responsible enough to take care of one
   c. I don't really like having pets

3. What role does your pet (or future pet) play in your life?
   a. My best friend
   b. My assistant (e.g., guard dog, service animal)
   c. No role (I don't have/want a pet)

4. How would you feel if your partner never wanted a pet?
   a. It would be a deal breaker
   b. It would not be good, but we could figure it out
   c. That would be fabulous

5. Would you ever give up your pet if your partner didn't like them?
   a. Never
   b. Maybe
   c. Yes, if it was necessary
   d. Doesn't apply

6. How do you expect a partner to treat your pet (or future pet)?
    a. Like a member of the family
    b. However they feel comfortable
    c. Doesn't apply

7. Do you believe that pets have a sixth sense about people?
    a. Yes
    b. No
    c. Maybe

8. If your pet didn't like someone you were dating, would this be a deal breaker?
    a. Yes
    b. No
    c. Maybe
    d. Doesn't apply

9. Is loving animals a prerequisite for being your partner?
    a. Yes
    b. No
    c. Depends on the kind of animal

10. Do you think that getting a pet with a partner is a good way to test the waters for having kids?
    a. Absolutely—you can practice divvying up responsibilities
    b. Sort of—but you can leave most pets at home by themselves so…
    c. Definitely not—kids are a totally different ball game

For many people, a furry friend (or two or three) entered their life before a partner. For others, having a pet is a must once they do meet someone and are ready to settle down. Others still may not want to have a pet—now or in the future. Make sure you and a potential partner are on the same page when it comes to having/not having a pet together.

Your Biggest
Fears, Dreams, and Goals

Write your answers on the lines provided.

Your most vivid dream or goal for your future is:

_____

_____

The thing that excites you the most about life is:

_____

_____

The thing that scares you most about life is:

_____

_____

The biggest way you doubt yourself is:

_____

_____

You're most grateful for:

_____

_____

You cheer yourself on by:

_____

_____

You'd feel _____ if you never accomplished
your major goals.

You'd feel _____ if you never found a **life partner.**

You feel _____ when you think about **growing old.**

If you never accomplish _____ ,
you know you'll regret it later.

When you spend your life with someone, you (ideally!) encourage each other to accomplish individual goals and dreams, and support each other in overcoming any fears. You might share some of your own hopes and fears in the dating stage to see who's up to the task (and who's not).

The Hardest Thing about Dating Is...

Circle the option in each scenario that resonates most with you.

It is terrible when you...

DON'T:
  ○ Have a good time on a date
  ○ Get to the actual date part

ARE:
  ○ Ghosted
  ○ Subjected to a brutally honest rejection

HAVE:
  ○ Too many prospects
  ○ Not enough prospects

FEEL:
  ○ Like everyone is playing the game
  ○ Like everyone is taking it too seriously

TRY:
  ○ To craft clever messages
  ○ To wait the "right" amount of time before texting back

CAN'T:
  ○ Find perfection
  ○ Find a deep connection

DISCOVER:
  ○ Taking the perfect dating profile picture is impossible
  ○ Someone looks nothing like their picture

FEEL:
  ○ Stuck in relationship purgatory
  ○ Ignored when you want to define the relationship

| FEEL: | O Like everyone is too jaded |
| | O Like everyone is too easy to replace or ghost |

| ARE: | O Googled by a prospective date |
| | O Unable to resist googling a prospective date |

| SPEND: | O More time on nuance and reading between the lines |
| | O More time choosing emojis over real words |

Many people gripe about how hard dating is—because it *is* hard. Knowing your specific pain points, however, can help you be more focused and up-front from the start, as well as less tolerant of people who push those pain points.

Meet Potential Dates:

Check off each option that applies to you.

☐ At work

☐ At the gym

☐ On dating sites or apps

☐ On social media

☐ Through friends

☐ Through family members

☐ At bars

☐ At clubs

☐ At coffee shops

☐ At parks

☐ At school

☐ At the farmers' market

☐ Through sports or other hobbies

☐ Through volunteering

☐ Through cultural clubs or events

Use your results in this quiz to evaluate how well different locations and methods for meeting people have worked for you so far. For the items you didn't select, ask yourself if these avenues could be worth exploring.

What Makes You a Good Partner?

Write your answers on the lines provided.

Your best quality as a romantic partner is:

_____

_____

You know you're ready for a serious partnership because:

_____

_____

You still need to work on:

_____

_____

You've done a lot of work on _____ ,
and you feel confident that you can continue growing by:

_____

You show that you're a reliable person by:

_____

_____

You show that you're a trustworthy person by:

_____

_____

You show that you're an empathetic person by:

_____

_____

You would support your partner by:

_____

_____

A love lesson you've learned that you'll take into your next relationship is:

_____

_____

The right person will be lucky to have you as a partner because:

_____

_____

There's a big difference between *wanting* to be in a relationship and being *ready* for it. Use this quiz to evaluate your ability to love and support another person *right now*.

Evaluating Your Dating Profile(s)

Write your answers on a separate piece of paper.

1. How would you describe your online/app dating experiences so far?

2. What did you make sure your profile included (e.g., a particular photo or certain anecdote about yourself)?

3. Why did you choose the specific photos of yourself that you posted?

4. How do your pictures represent the *real* you?

5. Is there anything about you that you purposefully didn't add to your profile? Why?

6. How does your profile capture your personality?

7. Do people you actually want to date tend to reach out to you?

8. Have you ever asked a friend to read over your profile and give you candid feedback?

9. How might your profile limit your options?

10. What type of person do you want your profile to attract?

11. If you haven't used an online dating site, why not?

If you've been in the online dating game recently, use your answers in this quiz to assess how well your profile(s) showcases your best self. Some people are reluctant to toot their own horns for fear of seeming overconfident, while others may be afraid to show who they really are for fear of rejection. If you don't have a dating profile but would consider trying it out in the future, use this quiz to consider how you might get started.

Use These Filters for Online Dating:

Check off each option that applies to you.

☐ Age

☐ Height

☐ Weight

☐ Location

☐ Family status
(divorced, has kids)

☐ Astrological sign

☐ Education level

☐ Lifestyle habits
(smoking, drinking)

☐ Religion

☐ Political preferences

☐ Relationship goals

Of course, there's nothing wrong with targeting the type of partner you know you want, but it's important to keep in mind that the more filters you use, the more you narrow your pool of prospects. And even though you may assume that you're only attracted to, say, passionate Tauruses, you may be surprised by what happens when you try to be a bit more open—especially about the more surface-level things. Use this quiz to think about what you're willing to compromise on, and what you're not.

How You Define the Relationship

Circle the option in each scenario that resonates most with you.

When it comes to defining the relationship, you...

PREFER: O Having an official DTR (define the relationship) talk
          O Continuing to see the person and assume you're together at some point

PREFER: O Asking friends for advice first
          O To just go for it

PREFER: O Initiating the conversation
          O Waiting for the other person to

ASK: O For physical exclusivity first
          O For full exclusivity first

PREFER: O To talk about deleting your dating profiles first
          O To go straight into the DTR talk

TALK: O After you've gotten intimate
          O Before sexual intimacy starts

TALK: O Over text
          O In person

PREFER: O Discussing long-term relationship goals
          O Taking things one step at a time

TALK: O Sooner
          O Later

PREFER: O Going public with your relationship on social media
          O Keeping your status private

DTR is a tricky thing, especially when it comes to online dating. There are so many options and few face-to-face repercussions for ghosting, covertly dating multiple people, or simply avoiding the conversation. But should you want to get to the next level of intimacy, this conversation is a must. Use your responses to get clarity on what you need when you decide to take this step.

How Do You Handle Potential Red Flags?

Circle the option in each question that best applies to you.

1. If they want frequent updates of where you are and who you are with?
   a. Bring it up
   b. Let it go
   c. Get out ASAP

2. If they push your physical boundaries?
   a. Bring it up
   b. Let it go
   c. Get out ASAP

3. If they won't make things official or go public with your relationship?
   a. Bring it up
   b. Let it go
   c. Get out ASAP

4. If they're secretive with their phone or email?
   a. Bring it up
   b. Let it go
   c. Get out ASAP

5. If they guilt you for hanging out with your friends without them?
   a. Bring it up
   b. Let it go
   c. Get out ASAP

6. If they're constantly critiquing other people's appearances?
    a.   Bring it up
    b.   Let it go
    c.   Get out ASAP

7. If they admit that they've cheated in a past relationship?
    a.   Bring it up
    b.   Let it go
    c.   Get out ASAP

8. If they never apologize when they've hurt your feelings?
    a.   Bring it up
    b.   Let it go
    c.   Get out ASAP

9. If they say all of their exes are "crazy"?
    a.   Bring it up
    b.   Let it go
    c.   Get out ASAP

Ignoring red flags can mean wasting valuable time that could have been spent finding someone who is truly worth the effort. Knowing how you react to different red flags can be a good barometer to how aware you are of potential warning signs, and how permissive you may be of behaviors that are worth a double take.

Follow These Dating "Rules":

Check off each option that applies to you.

- ☐ Always trust your gut

- ☐ Date one person at a time

- ☐ Play hard to get

- ☐ Don't ask serious questions early on

- ☐ Don't kiss on the first date

- ☐ Move on if you don't feel an instant spark

- ☐ Wait a few days after the first date before calling or texting

- ☐ Wait to have sex until the third date or later

- ☐ Don't date anyone a friend has dated

Look over which rules you selected in this quiz and evaluate how following these rules has worked out for you so far. Which rules fall in line with your current values? Which ones do not?

Who You Are in the Relationship

Circle the option in each scenario that resonates most with you.

In relationships, you...

ARE: O The more passive and go-with-the-flow partner
      O The dominant, driving force

ARE: O The fixer-upper
      O The one who does the fixing

ARE: O The romantic
      O On the receiving end of romantic gestures

ARE: O The steady and even-keeled one
      O The more volatile and unpredictable one

ARE: O Someone who initiates conflict more often
      O Someone who tries to keep the peace whenever possible

ARE: O Someone who voices every concern
      O Someone who keeps grievances to myself

ARE: O The more affectionate partner
      O The less affectionate partner

ARE: O The one who says "I love you" first
      O The one who waits for the other person to say it first

ARE: O Someone who tends to get bored easily
       O Someone who is in it for the long haul

ARE: O The one who can be clingy
       O The one who can be detached

Your dating past can have a significant impact on your present (and future). Use this quiz to look at how your past has shaped the kind of partner you would be today. Is this the person you want to continue to be?

Expressing Your Wants and Needs

Write your answers on the lines provided.

You feel _____ about voicing your relationship wants and needs.

You usually share what you're looking for in a relationship when:

_____

_____

If you're really into someone, you typically tell them:

_____

_____

You feel _____ when you're able to express your wants and needs in a relationship.

You feel _____ when someone you're dating shares their wants or needs with you.

If you want to get intimate with someone, you usually:

_____

_____

If someone you're dating initiates sex and you're not into it, you usually:

_____

_____

When you feel overwhelmed by someone you're dating, you typically:

_____

_____

If you don't feel a connection with someone you're on a date with, you usually:

_____

_____

If someone is disrespectful to you on a date, you usually:

_____

_____

If you feel strung along by someone or don't know where you stand, you usually:

_____

_____

From casual dating to committed relationships, there are many opportunities to voice your wants and needs. Knowing how and when you take advantage of these chances (or don't) can help you—and your future partner—when it comes to ensuring these wants and needs are met.

Physical Attraction and Intimacy

Write your answers on a separate piece of paper.

1. What physical quality (or qualities) most attracts you to someone?

2. What nonphysical quality (or qualities) most attracts you to someone?

3. What's your biggest turn-on?

4. What's your biggest turnoff?

5. How often do you initiate intimacy versus wait for the other person to?

6. How soon is too soon for intimacy?

7. How long would you be willing to wait to be intimate?

8. How often do you think healthy couples should be intimate?

9. How often do you prefer to be intimate?

10. How do you feel about intimacy if you or a partner are menstruating?

11. If you and a partner weren't on the same page about sexual likes, frequency, etc., how would you address it?

For many, physical intimacy is a big part of a committed romantic relationship. Having a solid understanding of what you want out of this intimacy, what it means to you, and what your preferences are will help you in finding a partner who's physically compatible with you.

Sexual Fantasy or Sexual Deal Breaker?

Circle the option in each question that best applies to you.

1. How do you feel about watching porn together?
   a. It's my fantasy
   b. It's a deal breaker
   c. I'm willing to try it

2. How do you feel about having a threesome?
   a. It's my fantasy
   b. It's a deal breaker
   c. I'm willing to try it

3. How do you feel about S&M?
   a. It's my fantasy
   b. It's a deal breaker
   c. I'm willing to try it

4. How do you feel about sexual role-play?
   a. It's my fantasy
   b. It's a deal breaker
   c. I'm willing to try it

5. How do you feel about being intimate in public?
   a. It's my fantasy
   b. It's a deal breaker
   c. I'm willing to try it

6. How do you feel about being intimate in a larger group?
    a. It's my fantasy
    b. It's a deal breaker
    c. I'm willing to try it

7. How do you feel about being intimate while under the influence?
    a. It's my fantasy
    b. It's a deal breaker
    c. I'm willing to try it

8. How do you feel about using a sex toy?
    a. It's my fantasy
    b. It's a deal breaker
    c. I'm willing to try it

9. How do you feel about anal sex?
    a. It's my fantasy
    b. It's a deal breaker
    c. I'm willing to try it

10. How do you feel about swapping partners with another couple?
    a. It's my fantasy
    b. It's a deal breaker
    c. I'm willing to try it

Use your results to determine your boundaries in the bedroom. While your opinions could change later, these fantasies and deal breakers, in particular, are worth thinking about in advance so you will be able to communicate them to a partner—and have fun in bed, too, of course.

Set These Boundaries:

Check off each option that applies to you.

- ☐ Limiting time with people who drain you emotionally

- ☐ Speaking up when someone hurts your feelings

- ☐ Saying no to physical intimacy when you don't feel 100 percent ready to proceed

- ☐ Turning your phone on silent at night so you're not constantly answering texts or work emails

- ☐ Confronting someone about frequently being late or canceling plans

- ☐ Removing yourself from friend- or family-related drama

- ☐ Keeping your work life and personal life separate as needed

- ☐ Asking your parent(s) or other family members to stop sharing details about their marriage or marital issues

- ☐ Recognizing that you're not responsible for other people's feelings

Setting boundaries helps you avoid feeling resentful toward—or used by—other people. While it can be scary to advocate for yourself and your needs, doing so will produce happy and healthy relationships of all kinds.

Intimate Topics You'd Discuss with a Partner

Check off each option that applies to you, and add your own options to the list on the lines provided.

- ☐ The things you love/hate in bed
- ☐ Your fantasies
- ☐ Your past relationships
- ☐ Your past sexual experiences
- ☐ Your first sexual experience
- ☐ Your masturbation habits
- ☐ Your pornography-viewing habits

- ☐ Your embarrassing sexual moments
- ☐ Any uncomfortable sexual experiences
- ☐ Any embarrassing stories about your body
- ☐ Any parts of your body that you are uncomfortable with or insecure about
- ☐ _____
- ☐ _____

For some couples, no topics are off-limits. For others, some avenues are intentionally left unexplored. Use this quiz to figure out where you stand on the issues that can be tougher to discuss, so you can set necessary boundaries with a future partner.

Vulnerability and You

Write your answers on a separate piece of paper.

1. What does being vulnerable mean to you?

2. Why might vulnerability be important in a relationship?

3. When do you usually feel most vulnerable?

4. Why might finding a true connection be worth the risk of getting hurt?

5. When's the last time you were vulnerable? How was that experience?

6. What's the scariest thing about being vulnerable?

7. What's the most rewarding thing about being vulnerable?

8. When do you feel most comfortable letting your guard down?

9. What makes you shut down emotionally or pull your guard back up?

10. When do you feel most connected to other people?

Being vulnerable can feel unnerving, but it's a great chance to experience true connection with someone. Emotional intimacy is a key part of a committed relationship, so if your results to this quiz reveal that there may be something standing in your way, take some time to explore this now.

Favorite Romantic Gestures

Circle the option in each scenario that resonates most with you.

You...

LOVE: O A bouquet   O A washed car

LOVE: O A home-cooked meal
O A table for two at your favorite restaurant

LOVE: O A love letter   O A love song

LOVE: O A sweet text
O A sticky note on the bathroom mirror

LOVE: O A surprise trip to a romantic location
O A surprise trip to a sports game

LOVE: O Something sweet   O Something salty

LOVE: O A picnic in the park
O Nighttime stargazing

LOVE: O A bubble bath   O A massage

LOVE: O A made bed   O Breakfast in bed

LOVE: O Impromptu cuddles
O Impromptu make-out sessions

LOVE: O Your favorite coffee drink delivered to the office
O Your favorite cocktail at home after work

LOVE: O Concert tickets
O Theme park tickets

Use your results to this quiz to uncover what makes you feel adored. A partner won't automatically know how to best woo you (at least, it's not common)—they'll know when you tell them. So, you'll first need to discover those acts for yourself.

How Do You Express Love?

Circle the option in each question that best applies to you.

1. **When you want to do something romantic for your partner, what are you most likely to do?**
   a. Spring for a hotel room and decorate the bed with rose petals
   b. Write them a love letter
   c. Buy them jewelry/a nice watch

2. **If your partner had a bad day, how would you cheer them up?**
   a. Encourage them to talk it out with me
   b. Give them a massage
   c. Cook them dinner

3. **What is your go-to, everyday romantic gesture likely to be?**
   a. Picking up my partner's favorite cereal from the grocery store
   b. Doing the dishes
   c. Tucking a sweet note into my partner's workbag

4. **What is the most powerful way to express love?**
   a. Through words
   b. Through actions
   c. Through physical connection

5. **When do you feel most connected to a romantic partner?**
   a. When we do something fun together
   b. When we stay in contact throughout the day via texting/phone calls
   c. When we hold hands, kiss, or are intimate

6. What would likely make you feel less connected to your partner?
    a. If they're on their phone while I'm trying to have a conversation with them
    b. If they make a negative comment about me
    c. If they turn down intimacy

7. When you want to express love, what are you least likely to do?
    a. Buy my partner something
    b. Tell them how I feel
    c. Be affectionate

8. Which of the following is a must for you to feel loved?
    a. Words of affirmation
    b. Physical touch
    c. Quality time
    d. Gifts

9. Which physical gesture means the most to you?
    a. Eye contact
    b. Hugs
    c. Hand squeezes
    d. Kisses

10. What do you most like to hear from a partner?
    a. "I love you"
    b. "Thank you for..."
    c. Actions speak louder than words

Everyone has their own "love language," or way that they express and experience love, whether it's through loving gestures, gifts, acts of service, physical affection, or quality time together. Your preferred way of showing and receiving love may or may not be the same as your partner's preferences, so it's worth understanding your own love language now so you can communicate it to your future partner, and in turn discover their love language.

To Maintain Autonomy in a Partnership, You...

Check off each option that applies to you, and add your own options to the list on the lines provided.

☐ Hang out with your friends without your partner present

☐ Travel with friends, with family members, or solo

☐ Volunteer with a cause you care about

☐ Work out, go for a run, or take a yoga class

☐ Nurture a passion

☐ Sign up for a spiritual retreat

☐ Stay in close contact with longtime friends

☐ Visit your relatives

☐ Go to happy hours with coworkers

☐ Set aside time to be by yourself

☐ _____

☐ _____

Look at your dating past and present: What passions and relationships have you held onto? What have you given up? Use your selections in this quiz as a guide for what you want to strive for in your next relationship.

Your Partnership Expectations

Write your answers on the lines provided.

You feel _____ when you don't get enough space in a relationship.

You feel _____ when a partner says they need space.

Your perspective about having outside interests and friendships while in a relationship is: _____

_____

When you hear statements like "My partner completes me," you feel:

_____

_____

You would feel _____ if your partner and you didn't share an activity or passion that you both could enjoy together.

Couples should ideally spend _____ percent of their time alone together.

You expect your partner to spend _____ percent of their time with their friends and outside interests.

You need your partner to be okay with you spending _____ percent of your time with your friends and outside interests.

You'd feel _____ about always sharing your location with your partner through location sharing or apps like Find My Friends.

You need privacy from your partner when:

_____

_____

Your responses to this quiz will help you gauge what partnership means to you—and how independent you think two people within a relationship should be. Ideally, you'll want your partner to have compatible views.

Why You're (Still) Single

Write your answers on a separate piece of paper.

1. Why haven't things worked out for you romantically?

2. To what extent have you feared commitment?

3. To what extent have you chosen partners who didn't want the same level of commitment or who had different priorities than you?

4. To what extent have you chosen partners who you felt the need to change or "fix"?

5. How will you give up unhealthy attractions or pursuits of people who aren't right for you?

6. To what extent do you need to break down your walls to let the right person in?

7. How may your standards be affecting your romantic journey?

8. How has independence played a role in your being single?

9. To what extent have you found yourself looking for the next best thing?

10. In what ways have you not been ready for a forever relationship?

Of course, there's nothing wrong with being single. It can be a great chance for self-growth and some much needed alone time. That said, understanding why you're still flying solo when you'd rather be coupled up can help you shift your relationship status to where you want it.

Feel Ready to:

Check off each option that applies to you.

- ☐ Spend a large amount of your time with one special person

- ☐ Share your living space with someone else

- ☐ Compromise to accommodate someone else and their needs

- ☐ Be vulnerable with someone

- ☐ Give up certain aspects of being single

- ☐ Love someone romantically

- ☐ Allow someone to love you romantically

- ☐ Be honest with yourself and others about your needs

How ready do you feel to not only have a partner, but be one yourself? And how ready are you to put in the effort to create a strong relationship? Use your answers to this quiz to gauge this, and determine whether there are things you may need to work on before coupling up.

What Does It Mean to Fall in Love?

Write your answers on the lines provided.

To you, falling in love means:

_____

_____

The idea of falling in love makes you feel:

_____

_____

Falling in love is exciting because:

_____

_____

Falling in love is scary because:

_____

_____

You'll know when you're in love when:

_____

_____

When you're in love, you feel:

_____

_____

When you're in love, you don't feel:

_____

_____

What matters most to you when you're in love is:

_____

_____

It usually takes you _____ (days, weeks, etc.) to fall in love with someone.

You feel_____when you fall in love quickly.

You feel_____when falling in love takes a long time.

Sometimes that feeling of love can hit all at once, while other times it can be more of a slow burn. Thinking about what falling in love means to you and how the experience manifests itself to you will help you recognize love when you do find it.

Finding Your Soul Mate

Circle the option in each question that best applies to you.

1. How much do you believe in the idea of a soul mate?
   a. Completely
   b. Not at all
   c. It's possible

2. How much do you believe that two people are meant to be?
   a. Completely
   b. Not at all
   c. It's possible

3. If you believe in the idea of a soul mate, what is a soul mate to you?
   a. Someone who completely gets me
   b. Someone with whom I have an intense physical and emotional connection
   c. Someone who feels like my destiny

4. To what extent are you looking for "The One"?
   a. That's what I'm shooting for
   b. This sounds unrealistic to me
   c. Ideally, but I'm not sure that's going to work out

5. Do you believe that you could potentially be completely compatible with multiple people?
   a. Nope, I'm just looking for "The One"
   b. Yes, it's just a matter of finding one of them
   c. Yes, but I'd settle for "good enough"

6. How perfect for you do you expect a soul mate to be?
   a. I expect pretty close to perfect
   b. A soul mate is more about connection than perfection
   c. No one is perfect

7. Can a soul mate have qualities that you dislike?
   a. For sure
   b. Maybe one or two
   c. Nope

8. What's the number one thing you need to have in common with someone to consider them a soul mate?
   a. Life priorities
   b. Values
   c. Our connection with each other

9. How will you know if you have found your soul mate?
   a. I'm not sure I will
   b. I expect to feel instant fireworks
   c. I expect to feel understood

10. What's a telltale sign that you've found the right person for you?
   a. A gut feeling that it's right
   b. A level of comfort around each other that's unparalleled
   c. A crazy amount of physical chemistry

Whether or not the term "soul mate" resonates with you, finding that right person is the ultimate goal of dating for many. Use your results to this quiz to help you uncover how you personally think you will know when you've found your match (however you define them).

Your Single-Life Bucket List

Check off each option that applies to you, and add your own options to the list on the lines provided.

- ☐ Live by yourself

- ☐ Live in another country

- ☐ Volunteer in another country

- ☐ Teach in another country

- ☐ Get a tattoo

- ☐ Travel alone

- ☐ Take a road trip

- ☐ Go on a big trip with friends

- ☐ Go skinny-dipping with friends

- ☐ Run a marathon

- ☐ Flirt with reckless abandon

- ☐ Have a one-night stand

- [ ] Learn how to fix things around your living space without having to call a professional

- [ ] Learn a new skill

- [ ] Get a pet

- [ ] _____

- [ ] _____

During your quest to find a forever partner, don't forget to live it up! Life should never be put on hold just because things in the romance department may be less than fruitful. You'll be sure to enter into your next relationship with zero regrets, and even with a better understanding of yourself.

Prepping for a Partner

Write your answers on a separate piece of paper.

1. What steps may you need to take to be ready to find and build a life with a forever partner?

2. Do you feel that you're primed to attract the type of person you ultimately want to be with? Why, or why not?

3. To what extent do you believe that someone can love and accept you as you are?

4. To what extent do you believe you need to change or improve something about yourself in order to build a life with someone?

5. To what extent do you believe that you deserve to find a partner of quality?

6. What loose ends (lingering exes, emotional scars, etc.) do you want to tie up before meeting the right person?

7. How much time are you willing to devote to working on yourself?

8. How much time are you willing to devote to dating and meeting people?

9. How much of yourself are you willing to give to another person in order to be a partner?

Preparing to be a partner means being ready and willing to put the necessary work into becoming the best significant other you can be. Use your responses to this quiz to gauge where you are on the readiness meter, and what may be left to work on before coupling up.

Part 3

FUTURE

Thinking about the future isn't about setting lofty expectations that you (or a prospective partner) most likely could never live up to. It's about defining the more specific needs and goals that you have going forward. When you truly understand what qualities you're looking for in a future partner, you are better able to recognize that partner when you see them and, well, go get 'em.

The quizzes in this part allow you to take all of the introspection you've done about your past and present, and use it to inform your romantic decisions from here on out. While you can't predict everything life will send your way, you *do* have the opportunity to manifest a healthy, happy partnership by understanding what that partnership looks like for you. Use your results to not only determine your values, goals, and needs, but also open the door to effective communication and important discussions about long-term compatibility.

Where You See Yourself in Ten Years

Circle the option in each question that best applies to you.

1. **Married?**
   a. Likely
   b. Unlikely
   c. It's complicated: _____ (explain)

2. **Kids?**
   a. Nope
   b. One kid
   c. Two or more

3. **Location?**
   a. Where I'm at now
   b. In the city
   c. In the suburbs
   d. In a rural/remote area

4. **Housing?**
   a. A house I bought (or bought with my partner)
   b. A rented apartment or condo
   c. A tiny house or #vanlife

5. **Car?**
   a. Leasing a new ride every few years
   b. Driving my clunker into the ground
   c. Biking or using public transit

6. Career?
   a. Changing my career or starting my own business
   b. Working in the same industry
   c. Staying at home (maybe with kids)

7. Retirement goals?
   a. Hustle and retire by fifty
   b. Leave the workforce at sixty-five
   c. Keep working in some capacity for as long as possible

8. Travel?
   a. As much as I can
   b. One or two longer trips each year
   c. Lots of weekend getaways

9. Still connected with current friends?
   a. Likely
   b. Unlikely
   c. It's complicated: _____ (explain)

10. Feel like you have life figured out?
    a. Likely
    b. Unlikely
    c. It's complicated: _____ (explain)

It's one of those questions that can really stump you: Where do you see yourself in ten years? While there's no way you can predict everything that will happen, outlining a road map of where you want to be will help you determine if a potential partner's plan falls in line with your own. A partner's plan may even compel you to change previous beliefs on what will or will not work for you.

Money and Your Future Partnership

Write your answers on the lines provided.

To you, being totally up-front about money means:

_____

_____

In a future partnership, you hope the person who handles the money is:

_____

_____

To account for your individual past financial decisions, you'd expect you both as a couple to devote _____ percent of your total income to tackling debt.

To enjoy the present together, you expect you both as a couple to spend your extra money on: _____

_____

To prepare for your future, you'd expect you both as a couple to save:

_____

_____

Your worst-case scenario for future finances would be if:

_____

_____

You'd feel _____ about having joint bank accounts with a partner.

You'd feel _____ about keeping bank accounts separate.

You'd feel _____ about asking to borrow money from your partner.

You'd feel _____ about asking to borrow money from either your parent(s) or your partner's parent(s).

You could see yourself hiding money issues from your partner if:

_____

_____

You'd feel _____ if your partner hid spending or financial problems from you.

If you overdrew your checking account, you would tell your partner:

_____

_____

If you had a money-related addiction—even something like too much online shopping—you would tell your partner:

_____

_____

If you noticed strange charges made by your partner in your joint account, or in their personal account, you would:

_____

_____

Being like-minded when it comes to money matters is typically a key aspect of a happy partnership. Use your responses as a road map for your financial future with a prospective partner. With a clear idea of how you'd handle these sticky situations, you can better communicate your stance on these issues—avoiding stress and potential misunderstandings later.

Your Romantic Travel Style

Circle the option in each scenario that resonates most with you.

When traveling with a partner, you would...

PREFER: O Couples massage   O Solo spa treatment

PREFER: O Plush hotel   O Cozy Airbnb

PREFER: O All-inclusive resort   O Backpacking trip

PREFER: O Blended cocktails   O Craft beer tasting

PREFER: O No set plans   O Packed itinerary

PREFER: O Snow   O Sand

PREFER: O Just the two of you   O Friends and other couples included

PREFER: O Golfing   O Kayaking

PREFER: O Tourist attractions   O Off the beaten path

PREFER: O Guided tours   O Free exploration

PREFER: O Lots of lounging   O Lots of sightseeing

This quiz helps you determine to what extent you'll be a compatible travel companion with a potential partner. Being able to travel well together is an important aspect of a relationship. Maybe you are looking for someone who has similar goals for a given trip, or someone who takes you out of your comfort zone. Either way, the right match will make your vacations feel fulfilling.

Personality Qualities You Need in a Partner

Check off each option that applies to you, and add your own options to the list on the lines provided.

☐ Communicative

☐ Diplomatic (i.e., handles conflict well)

☐ Affectionate

☐ Mature

☐ Empathetic

☐ Funny

☐ Self-disciplined

☐ Dependable

☐ Self-aware

☐ Patient

☐ Ambitious

☐ Confident

☐ Positive

☐ Emotionally available

☐ Emotionally stable

☐ Respectful

☐ Trustworthy

☐ Generous

☐ _____

☐ _____

While some flexibility is necessary, you shouldn't compromise when it comes to what is most important to you in a future partner's character. Use this quiz as a jumping-off point to create a clear vision of what traits you want and need in a partner.

Lifestyle Qualities You Want in a Partner

Circle the option in each scenario that resonates most with you.

You...

WANT: O An animal lover   O Someone who isn't into animals

WANT: O Someone who is comfortable around kids
O Someone who is apathetic about kids

WANT: O An outdoorsy type   O An indoorsy type

WANT: O Someone who has their life together
O Someone who is still figuring things out

WANT: O A globe-trotter   O A homebody

WANT: O The handy type
O The type who knows how to call a repair person

WANT: O A creative person   O A cerebral person

WANT: O A spiritual type   O A secular type

WANT: O A smoker   O A nonsmoker

WANT: O Someone who is curious about drugs
O Someone who says no to drugs

WANT: O A sports nut   O An art nut

WANT: O An avid reader   O An avid podcast listener

WANT: O A good leader   O A team player

WANT: O A risk-averse person   O A risk-taker

When you spend your life with someone, you want your lifestyles to be compatible. For you, this may mean having differences that balance out your lives, or having more similarities that you can share in. Focus on three or four must-haves on this list and use them to help guide you as you determine the right love match for you. (Also keep in mind that these must-haves can evolve over time.)

Qualities You Couldn't Handle in a Partner

Check off each option that applies to you, and add your own options to the list on the lines provided.

☐ Interrupting when other people are talking

☐ Always needing to be right

☐ Always turning up late

☐ Not making eye contact

☐ Checking their phone frequently when hanging out with people IRL

☐ Being judgmental

☐ Tending to be flaky

☐ Talking about people behind their backs

☐ Needing to be liked by everyone

☐ Only talking about themselves

☐ Displaying dishonesty

☐ Being condescending

☐ _____

☐ _____

There are some qualities that you can deal with, and some that are likely deal breakers for you. Know what you won't stand for right off the bat so you can weed out the people that—if they are unwilling to change— just can't work for you long term.

Date Someone Who:

Check off each option that applies to you.

☐ Has already been married

☐ Is in the middle of a divorce

☐ Has kids

☐ Never wants kids

☐ Has a different religion

☐ Has a different political affiliation

☐ Is younger than you

☐ Is older than you

☐ Lives in a different city

☐ Lives in a different country

Be honest with yourself in this quiz, and explore what possibilities may lie outside of what you've envisioned for your romantic future. You may surprise yourself—and open up your prospects as a result.

Physical Qualities You Prefer in a Partner

Circle the option in each scenario that resonates most with you.

You...

PREFER: O Long hair   O Short hair

PREFER: O Dark hair   O Light hair

PREFER: O Light eyes   O Dark eyes

PREFER: O A slim build   O More to love

PREFER: O Someone taller than you   O Someone shorter than you

PREFER: O A muscular figure   O A more soft-bodied figure

PREFER: O A hairy bod   O A smooth bod

PREFER: O Quirky physical features   O Classic features

PREFER: O Someone who's well-polished
          O Someone who's a little disheveled

PREFER: O Someone who smells like perfume/cologne
          O Someone who rocks their natural musk

Physical characteristics are often what first draw you to a potential partner. You may find that you have specific preferences in terms of physical attraction, or that something you initially thought was important to you doesn't matter as much.

Analyzing Potential Partners

Write your answers on a separate piece of paper.

1. How long does it usually take for you to size someone up?

2. How long does it take for you to write someone off?

3. To what extent do you wait too long to see if someone's right for you? Do you feel like you've wasted time doing this?

4. How do you feel about compromising on your ideal physical characteristics in a future partner?

5. How do you feel about compromising on your ideal lifestyle characteristics in a future partner?

6. How do you feel about compromising on your ideal emotional or personality characteristics in a future partner?

7. Which of these (physical, lifestyle, or personality characteristics) is most important to you and why?

8. What would you consider changing about how you size up potential partners?

9. What's the best lesson you've learned about how to evaluate what makes someone right for you?

Use your answers to this quiz to evaluate how you size up and weed out possible partners. There is a balance to be struck, and being too rigid or quick in your assessments could hold you back from finding a great partner. Understand what you might stand to compromise on, and what qualities you need to prioritize in order to feel happy and fulfilled in a future partnership.

Rethinking Your Type

Write your answers on the lines provided.

Your type so far has been:

_____

_____

You think your type would be attracted to you because:

_____

_____

You could be more open to:

_____

_____

You could be less judgmental about:

_____

_____

You could be more discerning about:

_____

_____

You could prioritize _____ more.

You feel_____ about giving someone other than
your type a chance.

You feel_____ about finding someone who checks
all the boxes on your list of your ideal partner traits.

   Your ideal type can change over time. In fact, as you grow and shift
throughout your life experiences, it makes sense that who you're attracted to would as well. Your results to this quiz can draw attention to any
biases you may have that could benefit from a closer look. Understand
what you're willing to compromise on—and what you're not—so you can
get clear on your priorities when it comes to your ideal partner.

Your Romantic Musts

Check off each option that applies to you, and add your own options to the list on the lines provided.

- ☐ Knowing we can count on each other

- ☐ Expressing lavish romantic gestures

- ☐ Giving and/or receiving expensive gifts

- ☐ Having a deep, loving connection

- ☐ Taking care of the other when they are sick

- ☐ Taking an interest in each other's interests

- ☐ Showing affection

- ☐ Talking highly of each other to other people

- ☐ Understanding each other

- ☐ Being vulnerable with each other

- ☐ _____

- ☐ _____

Romance means different things to different people, yet it's one of the hallmark qualities that differentiates a platonic relationship from a, well, romantic one. Use this quiz to uncover all the ways you like to experience romance so you can communicate those romantic needs to a future partner.

Your Ideal Future First Date

Circle the option in each scenario that resonates most with you.

When it comes to a first date, you would...

RATHER: O Set the agenda yourself
O Your date plans the get-together

RATHER: O Go on a hike   O Go out to a nice dinner

RATHER: O Buy something new to wear   O Wear your favorite outfit

RATHER: O Do more of the talking   O Ask more questions

RATHER: O Split the check   O Pay for the date

RATHER: O End the date with a kiss   O End the date with a hug

RATHER: O Stay up all night talking
O Stay up all night getting busy

RATHER: O Text within the next day or two
O Send some carefully chosen emojis right after the date

RATHER: O Reach out first   O Wait for your date to reach out

Before moving in together or even having "the talk" (you know: the intimidating "What are we?" conversation) comes the first date! Your results here can help you assess the qualities you look for in a date, from what is most important, to what you may be able to compromise on going forward.

Follow These Relationship "Rules":

Check off each option that applies to you.

☐ Don't go to bed angry

☐ Always be 100 percent honest with each other

☐ Don't schedule intimacy

☐ Fight—arguing is healthy

☐ Never take each other for granted

☐ Never stop romancing each other

☐ Don't let yourself go

☐ Be each other's best friends

☐ Put your partner first

☐ Forgive and forget

☐ Never bad-mouth each other

☐ Give more than you receive

☐ Never compare your relationship to other couples' relationships

☐ Build intimacy outside of the bedroom

The advice you get from well-meaning friends and family, as well as books and online articles, can get stuck in your head and compel you to act as you think you "should" in your romantic life. Use this quiz to look at the common "rules" you may have heard, and consider which ones reflect your relationship values, and which ones don't.

The Couple You Want to Be Part Of

Write your answers on a separate piece of paper.

1. What are three essential characteristics of strong couples?

2. What qualities inspire you (or make you jealous) about the couples in your life?

3. What qualities tend to annoy you the most about couples you know?

4. To what extent do you think you and your future partner should post about each other on social media?

5. How much literal space do you need from a partner? (Could you shower together? Sleep in the back of a car together while camping?)

6. How close is *too close* when it comes to you and a partner? (Would you share a toothbrush?)

7. How comfortable do you want to be around your partner? (Not wearing makeup, farting in front of each other, etc.)

8. How connected do you want to be to your partner each day? (Texting every hour, waiting until you see each other face-to-face, etc.)

9. When you think of your ideal partnership, what are you doing together? (Traveling, working out together, bingeing a TV show, etc.)

10. To what extent do you want your partner's friends to be your friends, and vice versa?

Everyone has their own unique idea of what constitutes #couplegoals. Determining what that concept means to you will help you get closer to finding someone who has compatible relationship aspirations, and is accommodating of your unique aspirations.

Spending Special Days with Your Partner

Write your answers on the lines provided.

You would love to celebrate your birthday by:

_____

_____

You'd want your partner to _____

for you to celebrate your birthday.

You would expect your partner to take a vacation day to celebrate

_____ with you.

The holiday that's most important to you is _____,

and you want to celebrate it by _____

_____

You'd want to incorporate holiday traditions like_____

_____

into your relationship.

You feel _____ about the idea of traveling or taking a vacation with just your partner on a major holiday.

You'd feel _____ if your partner had a different view on how much (or how little) they like to celebrate holidays.

You feel _____ about Valentine's Day, and you'd ideally like to celebrate it by: _____

_____

You'd want to celebrate relationship anniversaries by:

_____

_____

You feel that _____(You/They/We) should do the planning/ most of the legwork to celebrate anniversaries.

Your future partner will be a major part of every special occasion. But not everyone has the same level of enthusiasm for certain holidays—or the same ways of recognizing them. Use your results to this quiz to identify what really matters to you when it comes to celebrating special days. Do you want a partner who feels the same way? How might you best communicate these celebration desires to a partner?

How Much Do You Care about...

Circle the option in each question that best applies to you.

1. Climate change?
   a. A lot
   b. A little
   c. Not at all

2. The impact of human life—discarded plastic, food waste—on the planet?
   a. A lot
   b. A little
   c. Not at all

3. Religion-fueled war and conflict?
   a. A lot
   b. A little
   c. Not at all

4. Refugee crises?
   a. A lot
   b. A little
   c. Not at all

5. Poverty?
   a. A lot
   b. A little
   c. Not at all

6. Racial equality?
   a. A lot
   b. A little
   c. Not at all

7. Gender equality?
   a. A lot
   b. A little
   c. Not at all

8. LGBTQ equality?
   a. A lot
   b. A little
   c. Not at all

9. Unequal distribution of wealth?
   a. A lot
   b. A little
   c. Not at all

10. Homelessness?

    a.   A lot

    b.   A little

    c.   Not at all

11. Sexual misconduct?

    a.   A lot

    b.   A little

    c.   Not at all

12. Gun control?

    a.   A lot

    b.   A little

    c.   Not at all

13. Reproductive rights?

    a.   A lot

    b.   A little

    c.   Not at all

How you and a prospective partner feel about certain social issues may be no big deal—or a deal breaker. Use this quiz to figure out where you stand on these topics and whether it's important to you that a partner have similar beliefs.

Date Someone Who Disagreed with You on:

Check off each option that applies to you.

- ☐ Whether or not to have kids

- ☐ How to raise kids

- ☐ Where they stand on the idea of gender fluidity

- ☐ What kind of food you should or shouldn't eat

- ☐ What kind of medical treatments are effective

- ☐ How much time either of you should spend with family

- ☐ Whether vaccination is a good idea

- ☐ How to navigate emotional boundaries with people outside of your relationship

- ☐ What kind of relationship you should have (e.g., monogamous versus open)

- ☐ What constitutes drug or alcohol abuse

- ☐ What constitutes emotional or physical abuse

Certain issues can push your buttons—within a romantic union *and* outside of it. Knowing those issues you want to be on the same page with a partner about is essential.

Your Beliefs about Living Together

Write your answers on the lines provided.

You feel _____ about living together before making a commitment like marriage.

You would want to know someone or date them for_____ (period of time/up to a certain milestone, e.g. an engagement) before considering moving in together.

Living together would help you both find out_____ _____ about each other and your relationship.

The best part of living with a partner would be:

_____

_____

One drawback of living with a partner would be:

_____

_____

Before moving in together, couples should talk about or figure out:

_____

_____

When couples move in together, they should move into:

_____

_____

The ideal number of bedrooms in your shared home would be:

_____

_____

The ideal number of bathrooms in your shared home would be:

_____

_____

To keep the peace/make things easier, you'd be willing to outsource household responsibilities like: _____

_____

Moving in together is a significant stage in a relationship. Use this quiz to figure out your values surrounding cohabitation to help make this future step as seamless as possible.

Your Ideal Morning with a Partner

Check off each option that applies to you, and add your own options to the list on the lines provided.

- ☐ Scrolling through your phones side by side in bed

- ☐ Engaging in morning intimacy

- ☐ Your partner cooking breakfast for you

- ☐ Cooking breakfast for your partner

- ☐ Getting up and outside early for a workout

- ☐ Going out to breakfast/brunch

- ☐ Putting on your favorite morning playlist

- ☐ Listening to or watching the news

- ☐ Watching the sun rise

- ☐ Sleeping in for as long as possible

- ☐ Staying in your pj's together for as long as possible

- ☐ Taking a shower together

- ☐ Walking your dog together around the neighborhood

- [ ] Watching cartoons and eating breakfast with your kids

- [ ] Watching cartoons and eating breakfast together

- [ ] _____

- [ ] _____

For some, mornings are the best; for others, they're the worst. Since you'll be waking up together every day, you'll want to be ready to communicate your ideas of what an ideal morning looks like to you.

Common Issues in a Shared Home

Circle the option in each question that best applies to you.

1. How would you feel about unequal division of household labor?
   a. It would really bother me
   b. It would somewhat bother me
   c. It wouldn't bother me

2. How would you feel about unequal division of shopping for the home?
   a. It would really bother me
   b. It would somewhat bother me
   c. It wouldn't bother me

3. How would you feel about unequal division of costs?
   a. It would really bother me
   b. It would somewhat bother me
   c. It wouldn't bother me

4. How would you feel about one person doing all of the cooking?
   a. It would really bother me
   b. It would somewhat bother me
   c. It wouldn't bother me

5. How would you feel about a messy bathroom?
   a. It would really bother me
   b. It would somewhat bother me
   c. It wouldn't bother me

6. How would you feel about a messy kitchen?
   a. It would really bother me
   b. It would somewhat bother me
   c. It wouldn't bother me

7. How would you feel about a messy bedroom?
   a. It would really bother me
   b. It would somewhat bother me
   c. It wouldn't bother me

8. How would you feel about the act of forgetting to lock doors and/or windows?
   a. It would really bother me
   b. It would somewhat bother me
   c. It wouldn't bother me

9. How would you feel about one person never filling up a shared car with gas/washing the car?
   a. It would really bother me
   b. It would somewhat bother me
   c. It wouldn't bother me

10. How would you feel about one person inviting people to come over (or stay over) without asking first?
    a. It would really bother me
    b. It would somewhat bother me
    c. It wouldn't bother me

11. How would you feel about one person doing all pet-related chores?
    a. It would really bother me
    b. It would somewhat bother me
    c. It wouldn't bother me

Living with another person—whether it's a family member, roommate, or significant other—can be challenging if you have different ideas of what it means to be clean, or different expectations of each other. Your results in this quiz will help you uncover your own wants and needs when it comes to creating a home with a partner so you can communicate these preferences to your future partner.

Home Tasks You'd Gladly Take On

Check off each option that applies to you, and add your own options to the list on the lines provided.

☐ Cleaning toilets and drains

☐ Getting up in the middle of the night to take the dog out

☐ Creating the household budget

☐ Paying the bills

☐ Doing the laundry

☐ Doing the grocery shopping

☐ Cooking the meals

☐ Doing the dishes

☐ Mowing the lawn and otherwise handling gardening

☐ Decorating the space

☐ Handling all home organization

☐ Fixing things when they break (or calling the repair person)

☐ _____

☐ _____

Knowing what household tasks you're down to take on is helpful for showing your future partner that you can be a team player. Plus, it will open the door to a helpful conversation on what to do about the chores you'd rather avoid. What tasks might they agree to tackle? Where might one or both of you need to compromise on a chore you dislike?

What Are Your Thoughts on Marriage and Weddings?

Write your answers on a separate piece of paper.

1. How important is it to you to get married?

2. What does marriage mean to you?

3. Could you have a long-term relationship with someone without getting married? Why, or why not?

4. How long do you believe people should date before getting engaged?

5. What do you need to know about your partner before proposing or accepting a marriage proposal?

6. What should your partner know and accept about you before you would consider getting engaged?

7. How do you feel about the traditional proposal process (the proposer asking parent(s) for their blessing, etc.)?

8. How long would you want your engagement to be, ideally, and what do you believe is the point of being engaged before getting married?

9. What conversations about marriage do you feel you need to have with a partner before deciding to get married?

10. How do you feel about having a wedding?

11. To what extent do you feel that you and your partner need to be on the same page about wedding planning?

Marriage is one of the biggest relationship "maybes." Use this quiz to explore your own feelings about marriage so you can articulate your commitment goals to a future partner, and identify where you may be willing to compromise.

Your Future Partner As Part of Your Family

Write your answers on the lines provided.

You'd describe your family in three words as:

_____, _____, and _____

You would feel comfortable introducing a partner to your family if:

_____

_____

You feel_____about a future romantic partner joining your family.

Your_____will likely be the most welcoming to your future partner.

Your_____will likely be the hardest on your future partner.

You hope your future partner gets along with your_____ because _____

You think your future partner will blend right in with your family if they:

_____

_____

You think your future partner may have a challenging time with your family if they: _____

_____

The family tradition you're excited to experience with a partner is:

_____

_____

Your partner will learn quickly that your family is:

_____

_____

The one thing you worry about your partner noticing or knowing about your family is: _____

_____

When you and your partner create a long-term union, you don't just end up with each other: You end up with the family members you both have in your lives. Think about what this means for you. What ups and downs might you face in this transition, or even later on in your relationship, based on different family dynamics?

Your Ideal Relationship with In-Laws

Write your answers on a separate piece of paper.

1. How close would you want to be with your partner's parent(s)?

2. What makes you excited about having in-laws?

3. What makes you nervous about having in-laws?

4. How frequently would you like to see your in-laws?

5. How close is too close when it comes to your partner's relationship with their parents?

6. To what extent (and in what ways) could your partner's parents be a positive part of your relationship?

7. To what extent (and in what ways) could your partner's parents be a deal breaker?

8. Would you consider living with your in-laws or having them live with you?

9. How close would you want your families to be with each other?

10. How do you feel about splitting holidays with your in-laws and not seeing your own family on certain holidays?

Knowing how you feel in theory about different aspects of a relationship with your future significant other's family is valuable for developing healthy boundaries. Keep your answers to these questions in mind when you discuss the realities of your future partner's parent(s) (their relationship/personalities, etc.).

Your Wedding Wants

Circle the option in each scenario that resonates most with you.

When it comes to a wedding, you would...

PREFER: O To invite friends and family   O To elope

PREFER: O A big wedding   O A small wedding

PREFER: O A big venue   O A courthouse

PREFER: O Brunch   O Dinner

PREFER: O A traditional wedding   O A modern wedding

PREFER: O Loose purse strings
O A tight budget

PREFER: O A religious ceremony   O A secular ceremony

PREFER: O A bridal party   O No bridal party

PREFER: O An outdoor celebration
O An indoor celebration

PREFER: O A destination wedding   O A local wedding

PREFER: O A city/hotel   O A ranch/outdoorsy venue

PREFER: o A DJ   o A band

PREFER: o A honeymoon right after
        o A honeymoon sometime later

It's never too early to dream about your ideal wedding—if that is something you want. While your answers may be modified over time, it's worth knowing what kind of celebration speaks to you. This way, you'll be able to communicate what's most important to you about your future wedding to your partner, or why you may not want a wedding at all.

What about the Tough Stuff?

Write your answers on the lines provided.

You'd feel_____ discussing your biggest insecurities with a future partner.

You'd feel_____ discussing your partner's insecurities.

You'd feel_____ discussing your past (e.g., relation-ships, trauma, and moments you're not proud of) with a future partner.

You'd feel_____ discussing your partner's past.

If you were feeling unsatisfied in your relationship, you would bring it up with your partner by: _____

_____

If you were feeling disconnected in your relationship, you would bring it up with your partner by: _____

_____

If you were feeling depressed, you would bring it up with your partner by:

_____

_____

If you thought your partner was feeling depressed, you would bring it up by:

_____

_____

If you felt your partner was acting outside of the norm, you would bring it up by:_____

_____

If you were feeling worried about your partner's lifestyle choices, you would bring it up by: _____

_____

If you thought your partner had done something untrustworthy, you would bring it up by: _____

_____

If you did something untrustworthy and had to come clean, you would bring it up by:_____

_____

Tough conversations are an inevitable part of a long-term union. Being able to bring them up with your partner forces you to be vulnerable—which, if you have a strong relationship, should ultimately strengthen your bond. While you never know exactly how you'd react to everything that may come up, this quiz will give you a clearer idea of your ability to discuss the tough stuff. Are there ways you can improve on this ability?

Do These Things for Love:

Check off each option that applies to you.

- ☐ Move to another city

- ☐ Quit your job

- ☐ Marry someone who has to travel a lot for work

- ☐ LAT, or live apart together (i.e., committed relationship, but separate addresses), so you could both take advantage of career opportunities in different locations

- ☐ Give up a relationship with a friend if they didn't accept your partner

- ☐ Give up a relationship with a family member if they didn't accept your partner

- ☐ Be with someone whose family disapproved of you

- ☐ Let your friends set you up on a date

- ☐ Let your parents set you up on a date

- ☐ Accept and love someone else's kids as your own

The lengths you will go for love can depend on a wide range of factors—a specific person, a feeling of desperation, or lack of options, etc. Use this quiz to figure out how willing you are to get outside of your comfort zone or take a certain risk to secure the love you want. Is there more room for motivation toward getting out of that comfort zone? Are there instances where you may need to be more cautious?

Could You Handle This?

Circle the option in each question that best applies to you, and explain your choice on the lines provided.

1. Do you think you could handle taking care of a sick parent?

   a. I feel like I could handle it, because_____

   b. I'd feel completely unprepared, because_____

   c. It's complicated: _____ (explain)

2. Do you think you could handle the death of one of your parents?

   a. I feel like I could handle it, because_____

   b. I'd feel completely unprepared, because_____

   c. It's complicated: _____ (explain)

3. Do you think you could handle a serious illness diagnosis—yours or your partner's?

   a. I feel like I could handle it, because_____

   b. I'd feel completely unprepared, because_____

   c. It's complicated: _____ (explain)

4. Do you think you could handle the death of a shared pet?

   a. I feel like I could handle it, because_____

   b. I'd feel completely unprepared, because_____

   c. It's complicated: _____ (explain)

5. Do you think you could handle becoming estranged from your family—or your partner's?

    a. I feel like I could handle it, because_____

    b. I'd feel completely unprepared, because_____

    c. It's complicated: _____ (explain)

6. Do you think you could handle one partner getting laid off?

    a. I feel like I could handle it, because_____

    b. I'd feel completely unprepared, because_____

    c. It's complicated: _____ (explain)

7. Do you think you could handle having a lack of money/experiencing financial hardship?

    a. I feel like I could handle it, because_____

    b. I'd feel completely unprepared, because_____

    c. It's complicated: _____ (explain)

8. Do you think you could handle difficulties in having a child?

    a. I feel like I could handle it, because_____

    b. I'd feel completely unprepared, because_____

    c. It's complicated: _____ (explain)

Any long-term relationship will no doubt include some difficult times. Be honest with yourself about what you currently feel about these challenging situations and how prepared you feel you would be to weather them with a future partner. What steps might you take to be more prepared?

Becoming a Parent

Write your answers on a separate piece of paper.

1. How important is it for you to have a kid (or more than one kid)?

2. How soon would you like to have kids after making a solid commitment or getting married?

3. What are your primary goals for being a parent—or choosing to be child-free?

4. What excites you about having a kid—or choosing to be child-free?

5. What worries you about having a kid—or choosing to be child-free?

6. What kind of relationship would you ideally want to have with your kid(s)?

7. Would you consider having a kid before finding a long-term partner?

8. How do you think having a child (or not having a child) would affect your relationship with your partner?

9. How important is it to you that your future partner be a good parent? What qualities will you look for in this regard?

10. If you have a hard time conceiving/are unable to conceive, would you consider IVF, a surrogate, or adoption? Why, or why not?

11. What needs to be in place financially in order for you to feel ready to have a kid?

12. What kind of childcare would you ideally want?

13. How much do you expect your partner to split parenting duties with you?

14. What would you ideally do to keep your relationship strong amid issues such as altered sleep schedules and feeding frustrations?

15. How will you know when/if you're really ready for a kid?

Having a child changes everything. And if you want to take this step with a future partner, it's important to have a clear idea of your goals and wants when it comes to being a parent and parenting with a significant other. If you don't want to take this step with a partner, it is just as important to communicate your expectations.

Try to Save Your Relationship by:

Check off each option that applies to you.

☐ Talking it out—even if it meant having the same conversation over and over

☐ Making a drastic change, like moving to a new city

☐ Being willing to change

☐ Asking your partner to change

☐ Going to a rehabilitation center

☐ Asking your partner to seek professional help for an unhealthy behavior

☐ Going to individual therapy

☐ Going to couples therapy

☐ Going on a couples retreat

☐ Separating temporarily for space and perspective

The measures you will take in a relationship can vary depending on the situation, and who you and your partner are—as individuals, and as a unit. Use this quiz to explore common reactions to difficult situations and determine your expectations for yourself and a future partner in these scenarios.

Mantras to Keep You Inspired

Circle the option in each question that best applies to you.

1. Which mantra would you use when you feel like you'll be single forever?
   a. My forever partner is out there becoming the right person for me
   b. Being single is not about a lack of options—it's a choice I am making not to settle

2. Which mantra would you use when you feel overwhelmed or anxious?
   a. I'm strong; I've got this
   b. Life is too short to worry about what might happen
   c. I don't have to figure it out all at once

3. Which mantra would you use when you experience disappointment?
   a. If a door closes, I will stop banging on it
   b. I won't give up now
   c. When life knocks me down, I will get back up

4. Which mantra would you use when you lose track of your goals?
   a. I am more than the mistakes I've made
   b. I will begin again...and again, and again
   c. There's always a second chance to get it right

5. Which mantra would you use when you feel a spark with someone new?
   a. I will savor this spark
   b. Falling in love takes courage
   c. I will give in to the feeling

6. Which mantra would you use when your gut tells you something's off?
   a. I will listen to the voice inside of me
   b. If something doesn't feel right, it probably isn't
   c. I know the truth by the way it feels

7. Which mantra would you use when you feel nervous about a first date?
   a. Every date is an opportunity for true love
   b. If I am myself, the right person will love me for it
   c. Nerves are part of the process: I'm invested and I care

8. Which mantra would you use when you feel self-conscious?
   a. I deserve to love myself
   b. My amazing qualities outweigh the not-so-great ones
   c. I am enough

9. Which mantra would you use when you feel lonely?
   a. I am my own best friend
   b. Love will come when I least expect it
   c. Being alone takes courage

10. Which mantra would you use when you feel jealous?
    a. To compare is to despair
    b. Jealousy happens when I forget to value myself
    c. I will find gratitude in my own life rather than envying others

In order to stay motivated, you'll need some tools in your emotional tool-box. By choosing affirmations for the different situations you're most likely to face in love, you can remind yourself that you're worthy of connection—and find the inspiration you need to keep going after your romantic goals.

Finding Your Forever

Write your answers on a separate piece of paper.

1. Why is now the right time for you to find a forever partner?

2. What do you most look forward to about finding the right person for you?

3. What scares you about finding that person?

4. What outstanding worries or anxiety do you have about dating and finding the right person?

5. What will you do when you feel overwhelmed or burnt out by dating?

6. How will you stay inspired—and accountable—in searching for someone who fulfills your wants and needs?

7. Who in your life can encourage you and support your journey to lasting love?

8. How far out of your comfort zone are you willing to get? (Would you get on a dating app if you've resisted thus far?)

9. What would it take for you to decide to make that move out of your comfort zone?

This quiz is designed to give you that extra push toward finding your forever partner. By taking a reflective look at your emotions about love, and outlining what encouragement you may need to go after what you want, you'll feel equipped to get out there and start living your love story.

Index

About the Author

Natasha Burton is a freelance writer and relationship expert who has written for *Cosmopolitan, Maxim, Women's Health*, Livestrong.com, and Brides.com, among other publications. She's the author of *101 Quizzes for Couples, 101 Quizzes for BFFs*, and *101 Quizzes for Brides & Grooms*, and the coauthor of *The Little Black Book of Big Red Flags*. She holds a master's degree in creative nonfiction writing from the University of Southern California and lives in Santa Barbara, California.